SPEAKING THE WORD FREELY

Writing with Purpose,
Preaching with Power

Jerome F. Larson

TASORA BOOKS
MINNEAPOLIS

Cover design by Art Sidner
Interior text design by Art Sidner

ISBN 10: 1-934690-43-0
ISBN 13: 978-1-934690-43-7

Tasora Books
5120 Cedar Lake Road
Minneapolis, MN 55416
(952) 345-4488
Distributed by Itasca Books
Printed in the U.S.A.

To order additional copies of this book go to www.itascabooks.com

TABLE OF CONTENTS

THE PROCESS PREACHING SYSTEM

Acknowledgments

Many people helped me as I wrote this book. I want to say thank you to them and acknowledge my debt of gratitude for their help and inspiration. I begin with my wife Joanne, the English major, who never gave up on me. She guided me through the writing of both my doctoral thesis and this book. She was always there listening to my ideas and helping me get started down the path of preaching freely. Her gentle yet pointed critiques of my preaching helped me see the need for change. In so many ways, I owe all this to her.

When it came time to consider publishing my manuscript, I called on my college friend and English professor, Dr. David Wee. David gave me a short course in writing and guided me through 6 months of re-writes. The book improved a great deal during those months, and I have David to thank for that. I want to thank my first student, Pastor Rob Hall, who had the courage to try something new. Rob became my biggest cheerleader. For the last 20 years he has faithfully used this method in his ministry.

I also want to thank my friend and parishioner, Lynn Peterson, who kept after me to follow through on this project. She explained exactly what I needed to do to get this book published. She then directed me to the resources I needed to do it. As I struggled to get the book published, I received support and positive suggestions from Bishop Lowell Erdahl. I want to thank him for picking me up and re-convincing me that I was on the right track. When it came time to prepare the manuscript for publication an angel appeared in my life by the name of Art Sidner. Art laid out the pages, developed a cover and made countless suggestions as to how the book should actually look.

Finally, I want to thank my greater family. I especially thank my three children and eight grandchildren who have listened patiently to my rantings about the importance of speaking freely. They were willing to listen and to try my methods whenever they spoke publicly. They have been pulling for me and for this project from its inception. I am deeply grateful for that.

I have learned that it takes a village to write a book. I am grateful to all of you.

Introduction

THE WRITTEN AND THE ORAL WORD
– two very different language delivery systems.

For thousands of years the only language delivery system available to human beings was talking; the oral word dominated the world of language. Then, over the course of a few thousand years, human beings invented a new language delivery system for sharing their thoughts, ideas, information and feelings – the written word.

Several thousand years ago people began communicating with written symbols and drawings. The written word developed very slowly, but it eventually began to dominate human communication. As a language delivery system, writing had important advantages over the oral word. By writing things down people no longer relied solely on memory. They passed things down from one generation to another. People wrote down ancient myths, historical events and stories. They shared matters that previously lived only in individual memories. The written word also helped commerce and everyday life. Letters, orders, and other written communications did not depend upon the memory of messengers.

Gradually the written language delivery system began to prevail, and to this day it remains the dominant system. With the advent of the printing press and the education of the masses, reading and writing virtually exploded. Suddenly people of every class and economic status could learn. More importantly, the printing press enabled anyone to share ideas with others. If one could read and write, the whole world opened up in ways it never could before.

In the Church, this new language delivery system enabled parishioners to read and study the Bible. It also enabled reformers, like Martin Luther, to spread ideas and teachings throughout the land. The advent of reading and writing among parishioners transformed everything in the Church. As parishioners learned to read the Bible, the oral word began taking a back seat to the written word.

It also changed preaching in the Church. Pastors began writing sermon manuscripts and reading them to their congregations. Martin Luther may have been responding to this development when he said, "Where the oral proclamation of the Gospel ceases the people will revert to heathenism in a year's time. The devil cares nothing about the written word, but where one speaks and preaches it, there he takes to flight" (Meuser 41).

We know that Luther wrote what he called a "Koncept" or plan for his sermons. From this plan his sermons flowed with considerable freedom. This suggests that Luther recognized the importance of not using the written word in the oral setting of preaching. So, although he did not abandon the practice of creating sermons with the written word, Luther delivered his sermons freely using his considerable oral skills to their best advantage.

The written word and the oral word are two different worlds of communication.

The **Written** word is printed. It is produced by the hand.
The **Oral** word is spoken. It is produced by the voice.

The **Written** word is seen (visual). People use their eyes to read it.
The **Oral** word is heard (audible). People use their ears to hear it.

The **Written** word's audience is readers.
The **Oral** word's audience is listeners.

When pastors take a manuscript and read it to their congregations, they use a written word in an oral setting. This hampers their ability to communicate their thoughts in a powerful way. The secret to good oral communication from the pulpit is first writing a good sermon and then delivering it freely.

PROCESS PREACHING

The system described in this book for converting a written manuscript to a powerful and well-delived oral communication is called Process Preaching. Also, the term extemporaneous is used throughout the book to describe this kind of presentation. Extemporaneous preachers do not wing it or fly by the seat of their pants. First they prepare a manuscript. Then they use a certain kind of oral rehearsal to convert the written word to an oral presentation. Finally they speak their sermon freely.

Extemporaneous preaching is not just for the gifted few. Anyone willing to follow a few simple steps and then orally rehearse their sermon can do it. My goal in this book is to help pastors do this easily and to convince them of its tremendous value.

SPEAKING FREELY

Speaking or preaching freely is another term that I use to describe this kind of oral presentation. When we speak freely we do not simply read or recite a written text. Rather, we put into use our oral communication skills. Homiletician Dr. Michael Rogness has said, "The age of reading before an audience is gone" (91). I agree, and I believe that preaching freely in the extemporaneous mode provides the best option for replacing this long-standing tradition of reading sermons from the pulpit.

Chapter 1
Definitions

As I have said, Process Preaching is a system for preaching extemporaneously. Over the years the word extemporaneous has been defined in several different ways. For this reason, I will begin by defining the three basic ways or modes of delivering a sermon. These are definitions I will use throughout this book.

I rediscovered these definitions in one of my college textbooks, *Fundamentals of Public Speaking* (21). They remain classic definitions and the ones I use exclusively in the Process Preaching System. Understanding these definitions helps one better understand the goal of Process Preaching. I have adjusted these definitions so that they speak to the task of preaching.

FIXED TEXT MODE:
In this mode of preaching, the preacher writes out a full manuscript. He/she then reads aloud this written text or reproduces the text word for word from memory.

This is the way many people deliver a sermon or speech. They first write a manuscript and then read it aloud or reproduce it from memory.

I recently attended my granddaughter's induction into the National Honor Society. Several students gave short speeches describing the mission of the National Honor Society. Without exception the students wrote out their speeches and read them to the audience.

The guest speaker for the event also read a manuscript he had prepared for the occasion. This typifies the way speeches are given in every arena of our lives.

IMPROMPTU MODE:

In this mode of preaching, the preacher is asked or prompted to preach on the spur of the moment. He/she has little chance to prepare for this preaching assignment. If some preparation occurs, it is extremely limited.

Impromptu is one of two ways to speak freely without reading or reciting a fixed text. We all speak in an impromptu manner in everyday conversation and whenever called upon to say a few words on the spur of the moment. Terms like off the cuff, winging it, and improvisation describe this kind of speaking. Many pastors use a modified form of impromptu preaching. They study a text, think about possible illustrations of the text, go over it in their minds, and then preach freely without any further preparation.

Pastors do this because they know and have experienced the power of preaching freely. Parishioners are both inspired and impressed by pastors who can speak freely without using any notes. This has the result of encouraging pastors to continue impromptu preaching. Once they realize they can be effective by preaching in this way, they find it difficult to go back to writing manuscripts.

EXTEMPORANEOUS MODE:

In this mode, preachers build their sermons prior to presentation, but they coin their language in the act of preaching. Their preparation is often very extensive and painstaking. As a rule, it entails the making of an outline, the preparation of elaborate notes, and often the writing of a full manuscript. This is followed by much oral rehearsal. The final expression of ideas is left to the occasion. The preacher knows that not being chained to a fixed sequence of words allows him/her to stop and restate an idea, add an illustration or comparison, or define an ambiguous phrase. Thus the extemporaneous preacher, sensitive to the immediate responses of the congregation, does not freeze language prior to delivery. The sermon is given its final form during the act of preaching.

In the extemporaneous mode of preaching, the delivery of a sermon differs from both the fixed text and the impromptu mode. Extemporaneous delivery is a second way of speaking freely. However, it requires two additional kinds of preparation. The preacher first prepares a full manuscript or very elaborate notes. Then, before delivering the sermon, the preacher spends time orally rehearsing it.

This extensive preparation makes extemporaneous preaching more effective than impromptu preaching. At the same time, much of what fixed-text preachers already do happens for an extemporaneous sermon. They still do the exegetical study of the text, still choose a theme for the sermon, and still write a manuscript.

The problem with learning to preach in the extemporaneous mode is the difficulty in seeing how to go about it. Some instruction helps one learn how to preach in this way. In the fixed-text or impromptu mode, one can easily see how to do it. For example, in the fixed-text mode you think, you write, and then you read or deliver a memorized text. In the impromptu mode you think about a subject and then you preach.

Things aren't so simple in the extemporaneous mode. In this mode you think, you write, and then you need to have a method for converting what you have written to an oral communication. Many different methods have worked for making this conversion from the written word to the oral word. For example, some pastors re-write their manuscripts in the form of notes and speak freely using only their notes as a guide. Another method involves thinking through the sermon until you can speak it freely. Some pastors seem to have a special gift and can write a full manuscript. Then, without any more preparation, remember what they have written and speak their sermon freely.

These methods have worked for many pastors over the years, but they do not work for everyone. Relying on these methods has often lead pastors to abandon all attempts at preaching extemporaneously.

This was the case in my own preaching life. On many occasions I tried to preach more freely. I had majored in speech in college and knew the importance of not reading my sermons. In both college and seminary we were encouraged to speak from notes. Over the years I occasionally tried this method but with very little success. I even tried winging it, but couldn't manage to get new material into my preaching with this method. Each time I tried something new I could sustain it for only a short time. I soon returned to reading my written manuscripts. Eventually, I could tell stories without reading them, and I could preach children's sermons freely. However, I couldn't take my sermon manuscripts into the pulpit and speak them freely.

Then, about 20 years ago, I decided to try again to move away from reading my sermons. I searched through many speech books in order to find a way of doing it. Then I saw the above definitions. As I read the definition for extemporaneous preaching, one sentence jumped out at me. "This is followed by much oral rehearsal." I had long ago given up orally rehearsing my sermons. The only oral rehearsal I knew how to do was reading the written text over and over, but it never helped me get away from reading my manuscript. I also discovered that I could read my sermon as well the first time through as the tenth time through.

The words "This is followed by much oral rehearsal" started me on a search for how to do these rehearsals. I combed through the book where I found the definition but discovered nothing more about how to do oral rehearsals. Then I searched through many speech textbooks but found nothing on oral rehearsals. I decided to begin experimenting with ways of doing oral rehearsals. When I did, an amazing thing happened.

One day I tried a different way of doing my oral rehearsals. In the process, I stumbled upon what I now consider the best way of converting a written text to an oral presentation. It happened quite by accident. That day I did not read the text over and over again or try to memorize the text word for word. Instead, I read the first section of my manuscript to myself. Then, I stepped aside from the pulpit and tried to preach it freely. I could not do it. I went back to the manuscript and looked at it again. I underlined and circled key words, and I tried to preach it a second time. This time I could preach some of what I had written in this first section, but not all of it.

For some reason, on that particular day, I did not give up. I tried a third time. I read again what I had written, stepped away from the pulpit, and again tried to speak it freely. When I did, an amazing thing happened. I could now preach what I had written. I said things a little differently from how I had written them, and I wasn't as fluent as when I read my manuscript. However, I could speak it freely without a problem. This amazed me and continues to amaze me. It took three tries before I could preach what I had written. During the third run-through my brain converted what I had written to an oral presentation. This made it possible for me to preach it freely.

This kind of oral rehearsal makes extemporaneous preaching possible. Other things go into preaching extemporaneously. However, doing oral rehearsals is essential to doing it on a regular basis. The type of memory used to achieve an extemporaneous delivery through oral rehearsal is common to everyone. For this reason anyone who wants to can speak extemporaneously. Perhaps some prefer to preach in another way, but no one's memory prevents them from preaching extemporaneously.

Learning how to do these oral rehearsals makes extemporaneous preaching easy enough to do every week. A 20-minute sermon manuscript can be converted to an oral presentation in about an hour and a half of oral rehearsal or, as I like to call them, run-throughs. You could say that there is a trick to speaking extemporaneously. The only trick is learning how to do these run-throughs.

In chapter eight I explain in great detail how to do these run-throughs. In teaching Process Preaching to pastors over the past ten years I have learned that all pastors can preach extemporaneously if they know how to do the right kind of oral rehearsal. In the next few chapters I hope I can convince you to give it a try.

Once you learn to preach extemporaneously, you will have a new and very useful tool for your preaching toolbox. This can add variety and new life to many different preaching and public speaking opportunities. Once you learn how, preaching in the extemporaneous mode takes no more time and becomes no more difficult than preaching in other ways.

Chapter 2
Preaching as a Two-Part Creative Process

In the second half of this book I will explain in detail how the Process Preaching System works. Here in the first part I will explore the ideas that led to the development of this system.

The Process Preaching System combines two creative activities, sermon writing and sermon delivery. In the fixed-text mode of delivery pastors exercise creativity in their writing. In the impromptu mode of delivery, pastors display creativity in their delivery. However, when they speak extemporaneously they can exercise their creativity during both sermon writing and sermon delivery.

CREATIVE SERMON WRITING

Writing requires our full creative faculties. While writing we put our thoughts and ideas into concrete form in creative ways that communicate ideas and capture the reader's imagination. When we write we focus and try to avoid distractions. Good writers need and use many other skills, including a strong vocabulary, a good understanding of grammar, and a creative and fertile mind.

I believe creating a sermon begins with writing the manuscript. When we write, we express the ideas we want to share with our congregation. Until the moment of writing, these ideas may have been loosely connected and un-organized. The writing process enables us to put our thoughts, discoveries, and ideas into our sermon. Through writing the sermon, we can find creative, innovative, and unique approaches to a text or theme.

Writing a manuscript also helps us clarify and edit what we want to say in our sermon. Consider our sermon stories and illustrations. I once shared with several people a story that I wanted to use in a sermon. Each time I told the story I would forget important aspects of it or express myself awkwardly. Later when I wrote the story down, I noticed that I could tell it much better. Writing made me more sensitive to the story's issues, and I used better and more creative language. I could read what I had written and then improve the story several times. Later, while rehearsing the sermon, I could convert this edited and more creative version of my story to the spoken word. By first writing it down, I told the story much better.

Many pastors shy away from speaking freely because they fear they will say the wrong thing. Indeed, this can happen if we speak off the cuff in an impromptu manner. In the extemporaneous mode of preaching, however, this does not happen because of the rethinking and rewriting that takes place before we enter the delivery process. This editing distinguishes speaking freely in the impromptu mode from speaking freely in the extemporaneous mode. In both cases we are not tied to a written text. However, in the extemporaneous mode we only say what has first been carefully written, thought through, and rehearsed.

CREATIVE SERMON DELIVERY

Creative writing makes up the first half of sermon preparation. Delivering what we have written in a creative manner makes up the second half. If we deliver our sermon extemporaneously, we will be just as creative in the delivery of our sermon as we are in the writing of it. This combination of creative writing and creative delivery gives extemporaneous preaching its greatest strength.

I recently heard the director of a local art school say, "Art is all about content, but the content needs to be delivered." He said this to justify his unpopular insistence that art students must learn how to draw and sculpt, etc. Sermons are not necessarily works of art, but they are definitely creative ventures. This means that their content, like works of art, must be delivered well to be effective.

Creative content enters our sermons chiefly through writing. Speaking the sermon freely and using our best oral skills delivers that content in a powerful way. At its best, sermon delivery, just like sermon writing, should engage all of our creative faculties. Unfortunately the most common way of delivering a sermon, reading a manuscript, can be done without engaging our creative faculties very much.

Not so with an extemporaneous delivery. In this mode of delivery, preachers have a great opportunity to engage their creative abilities at two different times during the preparation process. The first one comes during the run-through process.

Here the preacher has an opportunity to adjust, add, or change things from what was originally written.

Speaking the written words freely during these run-throughs engages the brain in such a way that new insights or ways of putting things often emerge. When they do, they can be added to the manuscript. Then, during subsequent run-throughs, these additions are firmed up using the new and often more creative way of saying things.

A second opportunity for creativity comes at the moment of delivery. Although a sermon normally follows closely the path of the final run-through, it often happens that changes emerge at the moment of delivery. This could be because a preacher is "getting into it," or because the audience evokes or inspires in the preacher a slightly different way of saying things.

I once had a visiting African pastor preach for me. He spoke freely without any notes and gave, I suspect, the same sermon he had given many times before. After the service I asked him for a copy of his sermon. He said that he did not have one because he did not want to get into the habit of reading his sermons. He believed it would keep him from connecting with the congregation.

I agree with this observation. When we read aloud something we have written, we seldom connect with our listeners. However, when we write a creative and dynamic sermon and deliver it freely, our sermon connects with a congregation in a genuine way.

This illustrates the heart of the debate over sermon delivery. People understand that when pastors speak freely as the African pastor did, they connect on a deeper level. Their sermon seems more personal and heartfelt. When pastors read what they have written, they often seem cold and distant.

When pastors speak freely, they often receive very positive feedback from their congregation. For this reason some pastors have abandoned writing sermons altogether. They consider it better to preach whatever comes to mind, more or less on the spur of the moment, than read a well-crafted creative sermon manuscript.

The extemporaneous mode of delivery enables pastors to experience the best of both worlds. They can apply their creative abilities to writing a manuscript and then apply their creative abilities in the delivery process. In this way, they will produce a final product that is much more than the sum of the two parts. They will have delivered their creative and well-written sermon in a powerful and creative way. This, in turn, will enable them to communicate the gospel very effectively.

Chapter 3
The Written and The Oral Word

THE DIFFERENCES

Although writing and delivering a sermon both use creative language skills, they do so in different ways. The Process Preaching System recognizes this and addresses it by converting the written word to the oral word. This happens during the oral rehearsal portion of the delivery process when the preacher adjusts, adds, and otherwise modifies the written text. It happens again to a lesser extent at the moment of delivery. At these moments the written language of the manuscript is converted to the oral language of delivery. At the heart of the Process Preaching System is this process of converting the written word to a much more powerful oral word.

Read or memorized sermons do not communicate well because the language used in writing is designed specifically for a reading audience. Many homileticians today recognize the important differences between the written word and the oral word. Some even suggest that preachers should try to write "orally." This, however, goes against our training as writers. This means that a different, more natural way of converting written language to oral language would benefit our preaching.

The Process Preaching System offers us such a benefit, and it does so in a natural way as part of the delivery process. The conversion takes place chiefly during the oral rehearsals. As the preacher runs through what has been written, new ways emerge to express the written thoughts. This comes naturally because our brain knows what it takes to communicate an idea orally. When we give our brain the freedom to express orally what we have written, it will quickly find the right words for clear oral expression.

We have all experienced the power of oral language in an oral setting. For example, you may have attended a lecture where the speaker reads a written manuscript, but then thinks of something to add and steps away from the podium and speaks freely. I have literally seen sleepers wake up when a lecturer switches from written to oral language.

Some people believe that certain speeches need to be read because of their complexity and the need for absolute precision. However, the difficulty of listening to such a speech may well render it ineffective. Public speaking has very broad applications, but, by its nature, it often fails to relate complicated and elaborate data. I have found, however, that speaking freely does enable the preacher to take complex theological principles and relate them in powerful ways. This possibility exists because during the oral rehearsals our brains help us select words that make what we say clear and understandable to our listeners.

WHAT I WROTE AND WHAT I SAID

Recently I compared a sermon manuscript I wrote with a tape of what I actually said when the sermon was preached extemporaneously. In the following paragraphs I will compare what I wrote in the first part of that sermon with what I said after my run-throughs and the final delivery. The differences are quite surprising. I will compare each paragraph beginning with what I wrote. I will then comment at the end of each paragraph about the differences between them.

In paragraph #1, I wrote:

This past week our seventh grandchild was born. Before we had grandchildren of our own, I remember people telling me how great it was. However, no one could actually explain why. I don't know if I can explain it either, but I know it has something to do with hope and with the future.

What I said was:

This past week our 7th grandchild was born. Before we ever had any grandchildren, people used to tell me how great it was. They said it's really wonderful having grandchildren, but they could never quite explain why it was so good to have grandchildren. Then I had them myself, and I had the same experience, but I am not sure that even now I can explain what's so great about having grandchildren. It's very difficult. However, I believe it has something to do with hope. I think it has something to do with the future and this combination of hope and future that comes with having grandchildren.

Comments:

1. Notice that I said more words than I wrote. This may lead you to fear that you will become long winded and will need to write shorter manuscripts. Typically, speaking freely may add a few minutes to a 15-minute sermon, but probably not much more. Sometimes we add things, and sometimes we delete.

2. Notice that I used the word grandchild or grandchildren just twice in the written text and six times in the spoken text. When we speak orally we naturally repeat things. This much repeating in a written text would seem redundant.

3. Towards the end of my written paragraph I wrote "I know it has something to do with the future." I said "I think it has something to do with the future." For some reason my brain substituted think for know. I suspect that at the moment of delivery it seemed better to be more tentative about what I did or didn't know.

In paragraph #2, I wrote:

When I was holding that little baby in my arms this week I couldn't help but wonder what he was going to be like. Each of our grandchildren is special and yet so different from the others. You can't help but wonder what this one will be like. Will he be musical, will he be an athlete, will he be tall or smart or handsome? Will he be like my other grandchildren and love to go fishing with grandpa or spend a day at the lake?

What I said was:

This past week as I was holding our, our new grandchild and,

and looking at him I, I just had this feeling of hope for the future. All of our, and, and I had this wonderment about what this child would be. All of our grandchildren are different as all children are different, and so you wonder, is it going to be musical, is it going to be athletic, is it going to be tall, is it going to be smart, is it going to be just, is it going to, is it going to, love to go fishing like my other grandchildren with grandpa once in awhile? Is it going to enjoy a day at the lake as they do?

Comments:

1. In this paragraph I did a lot of what might be considered stammering. I said things like "our, our," "and, and," "I, I." This kind of broken fluency typifies oral communication. In fact it is an integral part of speaking freely. Although I did not do it in this paragraph, using "ah, ah" or "um, um" is also a typical part of oral communication. My wife often encourages me not to use "ahs" and "ums." She and most speech teachers certainly have an important point. However, during an oral presentation, "ahs" and "ums" virtually melt into the background. One night while watching the "Antiques Road Show" on PBS television I noticed that one of the appraisers said "ah" 14 times during his appraisal. When I mentioned this to my wife, who was watching with me, she said, "I didn't notice a single one."

The more prepared we are the better our fluency will be and the less we will say "ah" and "um." However, fluency in public speaking is highly overrated. Many times when we pause and stammer a little it gives the listeners a chance to catch up, and it can actually heighten our listeners' interest in what we say.

2. Early in the paragraph I started out saying one thing, stopped, inserted something else, and then picked up with what I had started. I said, "All of our and, and I had." After a small insertion I continued with what I had originally started out saying: "All of our grandchildren are different." This is typical of speaking freely. We remember something, stop what we are saying, and insert it. You might think that this hurts communication or that it bothers our listeners, but nothing could be further from the truth. People easily accept this kind of interruption.

3. In the "what will this child be like" part of this paragraph, I changed "will he be" to "is this child going to be." This change took place at the moment of delivery, and when it did the brain quickly changed the way the rest of the paragraph was said. "Will he be" became "is it going to be," because now the subject is not "he" but rather "this child." When speaking freely we make this kind of change without even thinking about it.

4. At one point towards the end of the paragraph, I repeated the phrase "is it going to" three times before moving on. I was struggling at this point to remember what came next; this struggle typifies speaking freely. I was probably looking off into space as I repeated this phrase; finally I remembered it and went on. When this happens, you can feel the audience pulling for you. You can struggle mightily, and people simply struggle with you.

In paragraph #3 I wrote:

I don't know the answer to any of these things. I do know, however, that whatever he is like, he will make my life better. It is going to be exciting and fun watching him grow up and indeed helping him grow up.

What I said was:

I don't know the answers to all those questions right now but I do know that, for sure, that this grandchild is going to make a difference in my life. I know that this grandchild is going to change my future, and it's all going to be for the better. I am going to have a better life because of this grandchild, and so when I, when I, think about the child, I think about the future, I think about all the hope.

Comments:

1. In the first sentence I changed "any of these things" to "all of those questions." Here we see the brain making better sense of things. I had just asked several questions in the previous paragraph, so to restate the questions rather than just "things" clarifies my meaning. I may have made this change during the run-through process as the brain came up with improved wording.

2. Once again, in the oral version the word grandchild occurs three times, but in the written version not once.

3. At the end of this paragraph I addressed hope and the future, thus bringing in the main theme. When you are making

an oral presentation to listeners you must be careful to bring them with you all along the way. Naming the theme from time to time helps people follow you.

4. My grammar and syntax suffered in this section, as it often does when we speak freely. However, if you have a good command of the English language, it should not be a problem. All the language skills you have will transfer naturally from writing to speaking freely. After all, you are the same person speaking and writing, so it is your vocabulary and your language skill that come out in both settings.

In paragraph #4 I wrote:

Having grandchildren causes us to gaze into the future. It also gives us a sense of hope for the future just knowing that these wonderful little children are going to be part of our lives.

What I said was:

Well, having grandchildren is like that. It helps us kind of gaze into the future. We begin to look at the future and think, what will that future be for that child, what will the world be like for that child, and it gives us a sense of hope. It does that for us.

Comments:

1. This paragraph concludes the first section of the sermon, so it came naturally to summarize the meaning or purpose of the section. It ends up similar to the third paragraph. Some of the same things are said, and the theme of hope for the future and how children can give us this sense of hope is restated.

2. The end of sections and the end of the sermon often take on a life of their own. You are bringing the point home, so you naturally choose words that do the job. Here again a speaker's words almost become redundant, but with a little different twist. It is all part of bringing the point home.

SUMMING UP THE DIFFERENCES

Even though I have been preaching extemporaneously for the past 20 years, there are still tremendous differences between what I write and what I say. What I write no doubt leans toward the oral word. Yet there are amazing differences because of the conversion that takes place during the run-through process and at the actual time of delivery.

During the run-through process we set loose our verbal creative juices, and when we do, amazing things happen. This comparison illustrates the creativity that takes place during the run-through and delivery process. When I had my computer do a comparison between what I said and what I wrote, it could find only one sentence, the very first one, which exactly matched.

People do not like to be read to on Sunday mornings because they are hearing written language and not oral language. Written language works best when people are reading with their eyes. Oral language works better when people are listening with their ears. Reading a sermon manuscript aloud communicates poorly. Conversely, you would never think of publishing word for word a taped transcript of an extemporaneous sermon with all of its oral interpretive quirks.

The written and the oral word differ greatly. They are both important and creative ways of communicating, but each has its own specific purpose. The most typical characteristics of an oral communication are these:

1. Repeating – In an oral communication a preacher often repeats words and phrases without sounding redundant.

2. Broken fluency – Sometimes we get ahead of ourselves and stammer a little to let our brains catch up.

3. "Ah's" and "um's" – When we preach freely these things occur naturally. Although no one recommends their use, they do not distract if used on occasion. Fluency is highly overrated.

4. Inserts – When we preach freely, we often insert things by stopping, adding a sentence, and then going back to where we were. This does not bother most listeners.

5. Stalling – Sometimes while thinking we will repeat a word or a phrase. We might also have what seems like an extensive pause while we are thinking or looking for something on our manuscript. This is not as big a distraction as one might think. The congregation simply thinks along with us and waits patiently – as long as we continue to speak freely once we remember or find out what comes next.

6. Changes – Sometimes we make changes during the run-through process or at the moment of delivery. The brain simply finds a better way to say something or to add another idea.

7. Repeating theme – Coming back to the main theme of a sermon or a section of a sermon typifies preaching freely, especially at the end of a section and the end of the sermon.

I realize that much of this runs contrary to our writing intuition and certainly contrary to our educational experience. It does not run contrary, however, to our natural instincts once we begin to speak freely. If we attempt to say freely what we have written without memorizing our text word for word, the things I have listed above will happen. It is not something we have to think much about. It is simply the natural result of speaking in an impromptu or extemporaneous way.

We already live in both of these verbal worlds. All day long we speak freely in our conversations. If you would analyze those conversations, you would discover all of the characteristics listed above. When we convert the written word of a sermon manuscript to an oral word for preaching, we simply make our communication more effective.

One of the most popular things in modern culture today is "talk" radio. In this format people call in with their opinions and ideas. The vast majority of these callers speak freely. They lack fluency and use all of the oral communication devices listed above. By speaking freely they communicate very effectively. Once in awhile callers will have their comments written out in full. They then proceed to read their comments word for word on the air. The result is totally ineffective. Although they are fluent, they are boring in the extreme. These callers think if they have everything written out it will be more effective, but the opposite happens.

The written word has a wonderful and invaluable purpose in our culture, but in an oral setting it simply does not work well. I believe that preachers must write sermons. However, reading aloud the exact words of those sermons renders them ineffective. Especially when compared to preaching those same thoughts and ideas freely. The secret to good preaching remains first writing a good sermon and then preaching it freely.

Chapter 4
Ten Reasons for Preaching Extemporaneously

Before pastors put large amounts of time into learning to preach extemporaneously, they will want to be convinced of its value. In this chapter I will give ten reasons why extemporaneous preaching is worth the effort.

1. THE TIMES HAVE CHANGED

We live in a time when people are growing unfamiliar with the art of listening. In the past, listening to long speeches was part of everyday life. The lecture method dominated teaching in the schools. Radio and TV stations broadcast entire speeches instead of 15-second sound bites. Even in the fields of politics and commerce, long speeches read from prepared manuscripts by officials were commonplace. In that kind of world, you either listened well or quickly fell behind.

During the past 40 years the situation has changed dramatically. We now live in a multi-media world of dramatic, colorful, and very effective communication. A typical PowerPoint multi-media presentation today includes full-color charts and graphs displayed on large overhead screens. Often dynamic audio complements video clips and still photography. Such a presentation appeals to all the senses of an audience. The listeners sit back, relax, and let the message come to them.

This also occurs in the world of television, where most people get their news and their views. In his book *Preaching to a TV Generation*, Michael Rogness says this about preaching to modern listeners: "The crisis of preaching is that we face an audience accustomed to new forms of communication. The way people listen is shaped by today's most dominant medium – television. We live in a communication world vastly different from that of our grandparents, and yet we preach about the same as preachers did before the arrival of television" (9).

By using teleprompters, newscasters and other television personalities, including television evangelists, can look the audience right in the eye while they read their scripts. In addition, because most shows are taped for later viewing, presentations are repeated until the presenters get it right. We rarely see live TV today. In fact, except for the news, live programs are so rare that they usually have the word "live" in their title.

Into this world of multi-media and teleprompted sound bites, we come to preach. Most homileticians today agree that reading sermons does not communicate well in this kind of world. Even so, I believe that public speaking in general and preaching in particular are not yet dead. In fact, I believe that extemporaneous preaching gives us a real fighting chance to compete in this multi-media world.

Hopeful signs of the on-going power of public speaking abound in the culture. For example, our local PBS television stations often broadcast programs that are nothing more than lectures spoken freely – especially during their pledge drives when they hope to bring in the viewers. I have seen many of these presenters several times now. They do not use graphics or multi-media of any kind. They simply stand up on a stage flanked by a few potted palms and speak freely. They talk about the meaning of life, how to make money, how to live the single life style, and many other topics.

These presenters always speak freely in an extemporaneous style. They never read their talks or have them memorized. The fact that they speak freely and use their oral communication skills makes them effective.

We see the power of oral communication making a comeback in other areas of modern culture as well. Recently I was reading a newspaper article about pod-casting. It mentioned a magazine for runners that published a pod-cast version of their most important articles. In these pod-casts the authors would deliver orally the information in their articles. One of the magazine's subscribers who listened regularly to these pod-casts said, "The written word is great, but when it comes straight from a person's mouth, it gives it that personal connection."

I note that churches that follow the church growth model of popular mega churches still place heavy emphasis upon preaching. The sermons are often given in a lecture style with Power-point and other media, but pastors speak freely without reading a fixed text.

The times have indeed changed: modern audiences cannot listen in the same way people did even 20 or 30 years ago. However, the power of the oral word in human communication is still with us. In every field of human endeavor, from politics to business to education, good oral communication continues to play a major role. In each of these fields the person who can speak freely on a regular basis has the best chance of communicating effectively. In the church good oral communication continues to make the Gospel real and alive for people. This is especially true in preaching as well as many other areas of church life.

2. THE REAL SELF EMERGES

When we speak freely we reveal our real self to the world. We are all different. We all have our own personality, and when we speak freely, that personality shines through. Extemporaneous preaching brings out each preacher's individual charm. When we read or recite a memorized text, this seldom happens.

When I talk about this in my seminars, many pastors have a negative reaction. After all they say, we are preaching Christ, not trying to charm a congregation with our personality. We know that if we are true to the Gospel, Christ must increase and we must decrease. This is true. However, we also know that Christ works through us in this world. Indeed, as the Apostle Paul says, " Christ makes his appeal through us."

In his book *Luther the Preacher*, Fred Meuser says this about Christ speaking through us: "Much is made of the doctrine of the real presence in Luther's sacramental theology. He also had another 'real presence' – the real presence of Christ in proclamation. When the proclamation about Christ is the biblical message of God's judgment and grace, not only is the preacher's word God's word, but when the preacher speaks, God is really present and speaking. In the sermon one actually encounters God" (13).

When I think back upon my own life of faith, I think of all the saints of God who taught and inspired me along the way. I can easily remember their wonderful personalities. I can close my eyes and imagine being in their presence and hearing their voice. Each of these pastors, teachers, and mentors along my walk of faith was distinctive. All of them had their own charm. Even though they had magnetic personalities, they always put Christ ahead of themselves. I never was tempted to worship them instead of Jesus Christ. I was attracted to Christ through them and by the dynamic way they shared their faith.

A speaker's individual personality and charm emerges in an amazing way when speaking freely. One of our local television reporters is stiff and dull when he reads his reports from a teleprompter standing in front of a camera at the State Capitol building. However, when interviewed on a local sports radio station, he speaks completely freely. He is charming and fun to listen to.

Another one of our local radio personalities who makes his living by being funny and charming has started doing radio commercials freely without reading a fixed text. His commercials are very effective because his humor and personality shine through everything he says. He and one of his partners often banter back and forth about a product. They are quietly cornering the market on radio commercials in our city.

We must remember that the personality that comes through when we speak freely helps us communicate. I realize that this may be a little intimidating to those of us who lack self-confidence. We may even think that we have to take on a substitute self in order to communicate in dynamic and interesting ways. However, we all communicate better when being our true selves. We are all unique, and the way we express ourselves when speaking freely gives us our best chance of getting people to listen to our message.

At the close of the Process Preaching Seminar I have each pastor preach the first five minutes of a sermon. I am always amazed by how unique and how effective each person is when speaking freely. Just hearing these pastors preach enables the class members to know them on a much deeper level. Speaking freely does that for us: it reveals our real self. This helps us greatly when proclaiming the Gospel good news.

3. EVERYTHING WORKS TOGETHER

Speaking freely allows our body and our mind to work together. This seldom happens when we read or recite a fixed text. For example, I once saw a very funny commercial on TV. It featured two men who owned a local building supply store. They would read a line of the commercial message and then add a gesture for emphasis. There was always a significant gap between the appropriate time for the gesture and the gesture itself. This made for some very humorous advertisements, although humor was probably not what they hoped to achieve.

When we preach freely, our body and our mind work together in perfect harmony. Amazingly, this happens without even thinking about it. Let me illustrate this by telling you about a pastor who tried the Process Preaching System.

Before this pastor attempted to preach extemporaneously, we video taped a sermon done in his current way of preaching (he was a fixed text preacher who read his manuscript). When we played this tape back, we noticed that his hands never left their grip on the sides of the pulpit. The only part of his body that moved was his head. It bobbed up and down as he tried to make occasional eye contact with the congregation. A few weeks later, after working through the Process Preaching System, we again taped one of his sermons. When we played this tape back, we immediately noticed that he gestured throughout the sermon and that his head was nearly always up and his face very expressive and animated.

The difference between the two sermons was even more noticeable when, quite by accident, we fast-forwarded through the sermons. When we did this, the second sermon actually looked like a scene from an old silent movie, with arms flying all over the place. It was hard to believe that the same person had done both sermons.

In viewing these videos you could tell that when he used the extemporaneous mode of delivery, gesturing came very naturally for this pastor. No one had spoken to him about his gesturing. Still, when he preached extemporaneously, his body and his mind came together, and the gestures simply flowed out of him in a natural way. This is one of the great benefits of preaching freely in the extemporaneous mode.

If you closely observe people who speak freely, you will notice that their gestures, facial expressions, and indeed their entire body language accompany their speaking voice perfectly. You don't have to teach people these things. I have a 3-year-old granddaughter whose facial expressions constantly amaze me. She can express hurt or joy or innocence, or anything she wants, without even thinking about it. No one has ever taught her what to do with her face when she begs her grandpa for something. And yet her expression makes her request irresistible.

It is almost impossible not to gesture when we speak freely. Recently, while waiting on a platform for a light rail train, I noticed a woman talking on her cell phone. With one hand she held her phone and with the other she gestured wildly. She didn't need to gesture in order to communicate with the person on the phone, but she couldn't help herself. I also saw a man talking on his cell phone while driving. I could see him gesturing with his free hand, and I wondered how he managed to steer the car.

When we speak freely, our entire body speaks. Malcolm Gladwell in his book, *The Tipping Point*, relates the results of a study that carefully observed and videotaped people in conversation. He says, "Condon spent a year and a half studying one short segment of film, until finally, in his peripheral vision, he saw what he had always sensed was there: the wife turning her head exactly as the husband's hands came up. From there he picked up other micro movements, other patterns that occurred over and over again, until he realized that in addition to talking and listening, the three people around the table were also engaging in what he termed 'interactional synchrony.' Their conversation had a rhythmic physical dimension. Each person would, within the space of one or two $1/45^{th}$ of a second frames, move a shoulder or cheek or an eyebrow or a hand, sustain that movement, stop it, change direction, and start again. And what's more those movements were perfectly in time to each person's own words – emphasizing and underlining and elaborating on the speech" (81)

All this happens naturally when we speak freely in our everyday conversations. It also happens when we speak freely from the pulpit. Our entire body conveys the message. When we speak freely, our verbal language and our body language work together beautifully.

4. EYE CONTACT / EYE EXPRESSION

The importance of eye contact when we preach cannot be overemphasized. Anyone who has taken a basic public speaking class understands eye contact. The ancient orator

Cicero, who enthralled Rome with his eloquence of speech a century before Christ, had this to say about the importance of the eyes in delivering a speech: "In delivery, next to voice in effectiveness is the countenance; and this is ruled over by the eyes. The expressive power of the human eye is so great that it determines, in a manner, the expression of the whole countenance." (Koller 35)

Good eye contact comes naturally when we speak freely in the extemporaneous or impromptu mode. Because we do not read a fixed text, we can look directly at the congregation. This is not the case when we read a manuscript. Our eyes and often our entire face are hidden from view.

I once served a congregation where the people were used to seldom looking at their pastor when he preached. The past several pastors had been fixed-text preachers, and the people evidently found that they could listen better without watching their pastor read his manuscript. When I began preaching at this church and looked out at the congregation, no one was looking back. Gradually, however, they began to realize that I was looking at them when I preached. By the end of the first month or so everyone was looking back at me.

We listen differently when someone reads to us. We can certainly get something out of listening to a fixed text being read, but we need to focus carefully on the text and work hard at listening. It may even be helpful to close our eyes. This means that eye contact between preacher and congregation is probably unnecessary when we read a fixed text.

When we talk about the importance of eye contact, we do so because the eyes, as Cicero said, are so expressive. I recently watched a John Denver musical special where he introduced a song he had written for his wife. He told how the words and music of the song came to him. He stood up to the microphone and stared off into space as he spoke. He wasn't looking at the audience, and yet they were looking right at him. They could see in his eyes and in his facial expression his feelings as he told this very touching story about how a beautiful song came to him. This eye and facial expression by John Denver was actually more effective than if he had been looking right at his audiance.

Perhaps the term eye expression describes more fully what takes place between an audience and a person who is speaking freely. Just as gestures come naturally to us when we speak freely, so too do eye contact and eye expression. Eye expression helps tremendously in communicating the words we speak as well as the feelings and the passion we have about those words.

5. WE MAKE BETTER SENSE

We discover when we speak freely that our thoughts must be well ordered and follow a logical progression. In other words, they have to make good sense. Our brain engages totally with our words and will not let us say senseless or illogical things.

When I first experimented with extemporaneous preaching, during the oral rehearsal process I discovered that my manuscripts had many shortcomings. For example, I would run through the first page of my sermon until I could speak it freely. Then, when I looked down at my manuscript to see what came next, I realized that what I had written did not fit. The process of speaking the sermon freely enabled me to see how what I had written did not follow a logical progression. Had I been reading my sermon, I might have just gone on and not changed a thing. However, because I was speaking freely, my brain would not let me continue.

Making good and logical sense is a principal benefit of speaking freely. It makes it easy to see where our sermon doesn't make sense or where we lack the proper transitions. This benefit soon drove me to become more organized in my writing. I learned that if I wrote a well-focused, organized sermon I could more easily preach freely.

6. SERMONS CAN STILL BE CAREFULLY CRAFTED

I recently had a student who wrote beautiful, "well-crafted" sermons. When she thought about giving up reading these sermons, she became concerned that her writing would not carry over to her preaching. Her language skills were considerable, and she put enormous effort into writing sermons each week. When she spoke freely, it surprised her to discover that her writing skills transferred over to her preaching skills. She could use her language skills to write beautifully and to speak beautifully. Her well-crafted and effective written sermon became a dynamic and effective extemporaneous sermon. The better we write the better we preach. Without good writing we will have little to say and will not say it very well.

Sometimes we write things we wish to say in the exact way we wrote them. We could memorize this particular phrase or sentence word for word. This takes a little extra time. Usually, however, during the run-through process you can get close to the exact words you have written without memorizing them word for word. Actually, you will deliver so much of your written text in a more orally communicative way that you need not worry. You can save the "turn of a phrase" for the many opportunities pastors have to communicate with the written word.

You will learn that even when you write something you consider great, it may not communicate well in an oral setting. You will learn to trust your oral communication skills. These will come to your aid mightily during the delivery process. You will see that a carefully crafted written sermon will become a carefully crafted and very effective oral communication.

7. IT'S NOT THAT HARD

Back in high school we had a choir director who had a favorite phrase whenever we struggled with a new piece. He would say, "Choir, this piece is not that hard. You can do it." The same thing applies to extemporaneous preaching. It's not that hard. Because extemp preaching does have a pretty steep learning curve, you may not believe this when you first start out. However, once you master the techniques for doing it, you will find it no more difficult to preach extemporaneously than to preach in other ways.

True, preaching extemporaneously presents some challenges. You must learn an efficient system that works. You could say there is a "trick" to preaching extemp. Have someone teach you how, and you can do it easily.

Growing up in Minnesota I once made the mistake of taking a sailboat out without knowing anything about sailing. The wind at my back easily drove me across a good-sized lake. However, when I turned the boat around to sail back home, I was stymied. I ended up paddling for several hours to get back. After that I didn't sail for many years. Then I met and became friends with a person who knew how to sail. In a couple of lessons he taught me how a sailboat works, and I have been in love with the sport ever since. Sailing is difficult to learn without instruction, even if you grow up in Minnesota.

In a similar way, extemporaneous preaching does not come naturally. However, with proper instruction anyone can learn to preach freely in the extemporaneous style. Extemporaneous preachers are not born but made. Everyone can do it with a little effort.

When they contemplate preaching extemporaneously, many pastors fear the extensive extra preparation time. Actually, the only thing added to a fixed-text sermon are the oral rehearsals. For a 20 – minute sermon the rehearsals typically take 60 – 90 minutes. Meanwhile you save time in the writing process because you do not carefully craft each sentence of your text. You will not say things in exactly the way you wrote them, so you can spend less time in the writing process.

Although anyone can use the Process Preaching System to convert a manuscript to an oral communication, it may come easier for some. Some people are very gifted free speakers. This comes from training, background, personality, upbringing, and perhaps most importantly, experience. This means that initially one person might complete oral rehearsals in an hour, and another might take two hours. Of course, the more we speak freely, the easier it becomes. I have taught this system to several hundred pastors, and none has failed to do it. We can all do it because we are all modern humans and our brains work alike.

8. IT OPENS UP NEW POSSIBILITIES FOR GROWTH

When we preach in the fixed text-mode, very little growth and development takes place in our delivery. Although we may improve our written manuscripts, our mode of delivery will remain the same. The extemporaneous mode of delivery opens up new opportunities for development and growth in our sermon delivery. By speaking freely we can enter a new era in our ability to present the spoken word. Shortly after I began speaking extemporaneously, I found myself trying new ways of preaching. We all want to improve our preaching, and speaking freely can literally jump-start our growth in preaching. It opens up many new possibilities.

For example, because you don't read your manuscript, you do not have to remain tied to preaching from the pulpit. In the chapter on delivery I explain a technique for preaching without notes and some guidelines for preaching outside of the pulpit.

An extemporaneous preacher need add only two steps to leave the manuscript behind. Remember, however, that the absence of notes is not what makes extemporaneous preaching so powerful. The power of extemp preaching comes from the oral character of the presentation.

Referring to your manuscript in order to see what comes next does not present a problem for your listeners. I tell my students that no one dislikes the fact that you check your notes, as long as you come back to your audience and speak freely. Now that I am retired and sitting in the pew, I actually appreciate the fact that my pastor refers to his notes. It indicates to me that he has prepared something.

9. YOUR SERMON SEEMS TO COME MORE FROM YOUR HEART AND MIND.

When you create a sermon manuscript, you put your whole self into it. You put your knowledge, your creative abilities, and your heart into it. When people read your sermons they see how heartfelt they are. Unfortunately, when you take this well-written and heartfelt document and read it to your congregation, it does not seem like it comes from your heart.

This fact characterizes public speaking in general. When people speak freely, everything they say seems to come from their heart. When they read or recite a text, it will not seem like it comes from their heart. I say "seem like" because the critical thing here is the perception of the listeners. Unfortunately, in this situation, we do not make the rules. We might wish it were different, but a sermon spoken freely will always appear to be coming more from a pastor's heart than a sermon read or memorized.

When I was a fixed-text preacher, I often had parishioners share with me their experience of hearing a pastor speak freely. They would say, "I visited a congregation last Sunday and the pastor was a wonderful speaker. She preached completely without notes, and you could tell it came straight from her heart." Often they said little about the content of the sermon. However, even if the content was limited, the sermon left a tremendous impression because it was spoken freely from the heart.

When we speak freely, what we say has a real impact upon our listeners. This has led some pastors to abandon writing altogether. Instead, they read a text and then say whatever comes to mind on the spur of the moment straight from the heart. They learn that many excellent things come to mind at the moment of delivery. This ability to come up with good material on the spur of the moment characterizes much human communication. Extemporaneous preachers receive this same benefit because at the moment of delivery they can make adjustments and additions to their presentation.

People in all walks of life have experienced great success when they speak freely from the heart. About ten years ago in our state we had a race for governor between two old-guard candidates from the Democratic and Republican parties and a third-party candidate. The old-guard candidates read their speeches and had memorized answers to most questions they faced. The third-party candidate never worked off a prepared manuscript, and whenever he spoke, he spoke completely freely. When the third-party candidate won the election it "shocked the world." I believe that he won because he always spoke freely, and what he said seemed to be coming right from his heart. People were impressed by this and voted for him.

Like this winning politician, we need to have our message seem like it comes from our heart. Our parishioners should feel that what we preach we also believe. Preaching extemporaneously enables us to do this. If what we write comes from our heart and we speak it freely, our intensity will touch our listeners.

Preaching from the heart also helps us put more passion into our preaching. Growing up in the Norwegian Lutheran tradition, I heard few preachers who put passion into their preaching. My seminary training, with an academic and scholarly emphasis about preaching, followed this tradition as well. Nevertheless, I still believe that passion plays an important role in orally communicating the Gospel.

Years ago I taught a confirmation class at 9:00 AM on Saturdays. Each Saturday morning as I stumbled out the door of the parsonage my wife would say, "be enthusiastic." It was hard to be enthusiastic about teaching a dozen ninth graders who always looked bored to death. However, I always put what passion I could into that class. Years later I spoke with a member of one of those classes who himself had become a pastor. He said he always enjoyed our confirmation classes. He said, "I didn't always understand what you were talking about, but the fact that you could get so excited about it made me think it must be important, and so I would listen and learn."

We may call it being enthusiastic or excited about our subject, but it all has to do with having a passion for what we try to communicate. The pastors and teachers in my life who have been the best communicators from the pulpit or the lectern were men and women who could get excited about ideas. It came out when they preached and lectured, and it came out because they spoke freely from the heart. Extemporaneous preaching can do this for anyone who wants to put some passion into their oral communication.

In addition, when we preach extemporaneously, what we say also "seems like" it comes from our mind. Following my oral rehearsal demonstration in a recent class, one of the students said that speaking freely made it seem like I really knew my material. It came from me and not from some other source. If we read a script, our listeners may think that we are reading someone else's material or that we don't know exactly what we are talking about.

My wife and I recently attended an orchestra concert that was preceded by a lecture explaining some things concerning the music and its composer. I mentioned to my wife that the speaker was doing a good job of speaking freely. Her comment in return was that he sure seemed to know what he was talking about. Because he spoke freely and did not read a script we knew that he really understood what he was sharing with us. It came from his mind and not out of a book or someone else's concert notes.

When I was a fixed-text preacher, a parishioner asked me if my sermons were sent out by the seminary. Even though I often shared personal stories about my family, some listeners still thought my sermons were someone else's creation. I believe that this would not have happened had I been preaching freely. The congregation would have seen that I was completely connected to everything I said. They would have realized that what they were hearing came out of my mind and not someone else's.

10. THERE IS A GROWING INTEREST FOR WHAT IS REAL.

Lately I have noticed an increased interest in things that are real. I think of the popularity of singers who can actually sing. I once heard someone refer to the jazz singer, Nora Jones, as the anti-Brittney. In concert she sang her songs instead of lip-syncing them. Recently the singer Josh Groban had an hour-long TV special in which he sang one incredible song after another with little help from an accompanying orchestra. The popular TV program American Idol searches the country for people with good voices. In their initial tryouts they have to stand before the judges and sing a song of their choice without accompaniment. Everyone who gets into the finals of this competition can sing. As the saying goes, "They are the real thing."

Reality TV shows are also extremely popular in our culture. One sees real people having real conversations in real life on these shows. You would think audiences would get bored watching such shows, but they don't. Every week a new type of reality show comes on the air.

When we preach on Sunday morning, we may think we need to jazz up our sermons with slides, videos, or special music. Not so. In fact, the world around us is once again looking for reality. Preaching freely in the extemporaneous style gives us the opportunity to embody reality to people looking for reality in an often very unreal world.

I hope this list of ten reasons for preaching extemporaneously will help convince you that preaching freely rewards the effort. True, we live in a day when our parishioners face all kinds of new communication technologies. Still, in every arena of life, basic oral communication not only survives but continues to thrive.

Here in Minnesota we have a professional storyteller named Kevin Kling who recently summed up the difference among the various media that compete for our attention. He said, "When you go to a movie, the audience stares at the screen. When you're acting in a play, the energy is exchanged between the performers. But when you're telling stories, 100 percent of the energy is exchanged back and forth with the audience." Then he adds, "To me, there's no better way to truly live in the moment. I just love the job of storytelling because it goes back to where you're from, what's funny, what's sacred, and it's all tied in to how you fit in your world" (A1).

Kevin Kling tells stories and draws large crowds at festivals all over the country. People are still attracted to powerful oral communication. Nothing will ever stop people from orally communicating with one another. As preachers, making our oral communications as dynamic and powerful as we can, will serve both our congregations and the Gospel well. Speaking freely in the extemporaneous mode gives us the best chance of doing this.

THE PROCESS PREACHING SYSTEM

Chapter 5
Introducing the System

When I was in college we experienced the traditional method of learning extemporaneous speaking. We had to write a full manuscript, outline this manuscript, and put the outline on note cards. We could take only these note cards with us to the lectern. The less we used these notes, the better grade we received. The professor wanted us to speak as freely as possible. This system prevented a student from simply reading a manuscript.

One of my college speech professors often told students in our class that a speech is not an essay on its hind legs. She believed that the best way to give a speech was to speak extemporaneously. She didn't focus on the differences between reading speeches and speaking them freely, but she made it clear that she wanted us always to speak freely.

When I went to the seminary our homiletics professor taught this same method of delivery. We had to write a manuscript, but he expected us to preach from notes without reading them. I had great difficulty doing this. One day I walked back from chapel with my homiletics professor and quizzed him about how he could preach so freely. He had just preached at the chapel service and had spoken freely throughout his sermon.

He had referred to his notes only rarely. He answered by saying he would look at what he wrote, circle a few key words, and perhaps check his manuscript for a starting sentence. He said this would "prime his pump" and he would just go from there.

When I tried to do what he could do easily, I couldn't do it. I could not look at a few circled notes or sentences and speak freely the rest of what I had written. I know now that he had a special gift for doing this. The way he accomplished preaching his sermons freely did not work for everyone. Throughout the first 25 years of my career I tried with little success to preach freely. After awhile I could tell stories freely and also retell the text freely. A few times I tried to preach from note cards, but using this method I never could consistently speak freely.

I began asking pastors who spoke freely how they managed to do it. I also read every book I could find that emphasized the importance of speaking freely. I discovered that all those who preach freely have their own way of doing it. But what helped them speak freely did not enable me to do so.

Several authors, however, steered me in the right direction. For example Ken Davis, in his book, *Secrets of Dynamic Communication,* indicates that the key is having a focus for the sermon. His book helped me see the importance of purpose and focus in extemporaneous preaching. Lowell Erdahl, in his book, *Preaching for the People,* shares a system for organizing a sermon into "chunks of thought," which he considered a key ingredient to preaching freely. Hugh Litchfield, in his book

Visualizing the Sermon, explains a system for connecting the brain to the manuscript so that it can be spoken freely.

The Process Preaching System has all these elements within it. I have added a particular kind of oral rehearsal. Once I learned how to do the oral rehearsals, these other things became part of a three-part system.

The three parts of the Process Preaching System:
   1. Purpose – Speaking freely relies upon a clear and well-written purpose.
   2. Writing – The sermon emerges during the writing process.
   3. Oral Rehearsal / Delivery – Oral rehearsal is the key to preaching freely in the extemporaneous mode. With a workable method for converting the written word to an oral word, Process Preaching makes extemporaneous preaching possible for everyone.

If you have a clear focus for your sermon, write it in an orderly way, and spend an hour or so in a certain kind of oral rehearsal. Then you can speak freely in the extemporaneous mode. In the next three chapters I will explain more fully how each of these parts of the Process Preaching System work.

Chapter 6
Process #1 - Purpose

The Process Preaching System begins with the writing of a purpose statement. A clear and focused purpose makes possible easier writing and delivery.

THE IMPORTANCE OF PURPOSE_

The importance of focus and purpose in sermon writing has come in and out of favor with homileticians. Martin Luther believed in the importance of focus. Fred Meuser writes about Luther's emphasis of having a key thought for a sermon: "Luther's method is to take a given segment of scripture, find the key thought within it, and make that unmistakably clear. The main point of a sermon is to be so clear in the preacher's mind that it controls everything that is said. If that is clear, then the rest of the sermon may be allowed to flow with considerable freedom" (47).

In the 1970's and early 80's, non-directional preaching became popular. Pastors simply expressed their thoughts about a text and let the listeners create their own sermon. Each listener might come away with a different point. This approach was probably an over-reaction to the earlier idea that a sermon should always have a theme and three points.

Recently we have seen a renewed attention to focus and purpose in sermon writing. For instance, Ken Davis writes: " I believe so strongly in the power of focus, I am convinced that any concerted effort to keep a sermon confined to a single objective will dramatically improve communication, even if that is the only effort made. I am equally convinced that the lack of such effort does more to destroy communication than any other single factor" (21).

Homiletician Hugh Litchfield also believes strongly in the importance of focus. He compares establishing a clear sermon focus with choosing a destination before beginning a trip. He writes: "Imagine asking people where they were going on their trip and they said, 'We're just going to start out and see where it takes us.' We might think that strange! It reminds us of the old adage that if you don't know where you're going, you're probably not going to get there. Have you ever heard sermons like that? The preacher starts out and lets the sermon go where it will. Most of the time, it never seems to arrive anywhere. It just goes here and there. Focused trips have destinations. So do focused sermons. There is a beginning and an ending. Before we get on the road, we plan on where we will get off it. The trip has purpose, destination" (21).

After I started preaching more focused sermons a parishioner told me, "Pastor, I followed you all the way through that sermon. I never got lost or had my mind wander while you were preaching." I still consider this one of the finest compliments I have received along my preaching journey. It helped me to know that someone completely followed what I said. In this chapter, I will outline a system that I have found helpful for developing focus and purpose in sermons.

DEVELOPING A SERMON'S PURPOSE

In the extemporaneous mode of preaching, clear purpose is essential. If you don't know your destination, you will have difficulty speaking freely in the extemporaneous mode. When you speak freely, the brain completely connects to your words. If the sermon lacks direction, frustration quickly sets in.

PRELIMINARY WORK

Developing a purpose grows out of the preliminary work done on a sermon. We all have our own way of doing the preliminaries. The typical steps include:

1. Exegesis – Most sermons begin with the study of a biblical text: translating the text from the original language, reviewing the historical context, and then living awhile with the text. During this process, Thomas Long writes, the preacher "follows hunches, explores possible avenues of meaning, and puts together clues on the way toward interpreting the text" (81). These hunches and clues will eventually provide the basis for your purpose statement.

2. Text study groups - Often pastors meet together to share and develop textual insights. These groups often help us understand a text's message. When we hear other pastors share what they have discovered in studying a text, it gets our creative juices going. Text study groups are a great way to begin focusing our thoughts on a text.

3. Commentaries - Many pastors read commentaries to see what others have discovered about a particular text. Thomas Long suggests this as the final piece, not an early piece, in the preparation process. He recommends it for comparing our interpretation with the historical interpretations of the Christian community. He believes that preparation begun with the reading of commentaries often stifles the creative process (76).

4. The Internet – In the past 15 years the sermon preparation resources available to pastors on the internet have expanded exponentially. These sites are particularly helpful if pastors wish to dialog about textual interpretations. Too much dependence on internet sites, however, can also stifle creativity.

5. One-on-One - The best way to gain focus for a particular sermon comes from meeting with one other pastor to discuss the text and its possible interpretations. When two people meet, they both are totally involved and committed to the conversation. An hour discussing a text with a fellow pastor can produce tremendous results. In larger groups your mind can wander when other people speak.

Try to find another pastor who preaches when you do and desires this kind of dialog. During my last eight years of parish ministry I preached every Sunday, as did a neighboring pastor friend. We worked together on our sermons every week for about an hour either in person or over the phone. We scheduled our conversation for mid-week so that we had both done our own exegesis and independent study of the text.

During our conversations, the creative sparks would literally fly. One-on-one conversations do that for us. They get our creative juices going as one person's comments spark an idea in the other person. After we talked for an hour or so about the text, we would begin to work on a purpose statement for the sermon. We always wrote out a purpose statement, and nine times out of ten our sermons shared the same purpose.

When Sunday was over, we often checked back with each other to see what the other person preached. Although we shared our ideas about the text and usually decided on the same purpose, our sermons always turned out differently.

I remember him sharing a story with me that we both eventually used in our sermons. For years he had fished in the Baptism River on the North Shore of Lake Superior. He would always park his car a mile or so from the river because there was a locked gate across the road. One year he asked the local game warden if he could get the gate opened so he wouldn't have to carry his gear so far. The warden said, "Oh, you never noticed that the gate isn't actually locked. That chain is just hanging there to make it look locked. It discourages 4-wheelers from tearing up the road. You can open it any time you want to go fishing."

In our sermons we used this story quite differently. He focused on not noticing that the gate was locked, and I used the story to illustrate the idea that the door to salvation is never locked.

I cannot emphasize enough the benefit of meeting with one other person to work on a sermon. Everything else you do to get ready to preach comes into focus during a one-on-one session.

The importance of a written purpose statement

Some pastors may be able to keep the focus of their sermon in mind without writing a purpose statement. However, I recommend writing both a general and a specific purpose statement for each sermon. Writing always gets the creative juices flowing, and writing a purpose statement begins the process of creating a sermon. Disciplining yourself to write one for every sermon will help in both the writing and the delivery process.

Two statements or one?

Many homileticians today believe that sermons need both a general and a specific purpose statement. Hugh Litchfield calls these statements the "General Objective (The City)" and the "Specific Objective (The House)." Thomas Long uses the terms "Focus" and "Function," and Ken Davis calls them the "Central Theme" and the "Proposition."

In the Process Preaching System the term "Faith Statement" describes the broadest goal for the sermon. The term "Purpose

Statement" describes the specific purpose. Whatever we name these statements, writing them holds the key to a well-focused sermon. For the extemporaneous preacher they are especially important.

Getting started

One begins the purpose statement writing process by asking the question, "Why am I preaching this sermon?" You may be looking for a specific reaction from your hearers, or you may want to have a particular effect upon them. For example, you may want to:

1. Convert your hearers to faith in Jesus Christ. This has been an important purpose for preaching since the time of Christ.

2. Strengthen or renew the faith they already have.

3. Inspire them in some way and for some purpose (evangelism, mission work, social ministry efforts, etc.)

4. Comfort them with the Gospel. (funerals, times of tragedy)

5. Change their minds or attitudes, persuade them.

6. Inform, enlighten, or guide them in some way.

These are a few of the possible reasons for preaching. In order to accomplish any of these things in a sermon, you will need a clear purpose. Asking the question, "Why am I preaching this sermon?" enables you to begin focusing your thoughts around a single purpose.

WRITING A FAITH STATEMENT

Writing a faith statement begins the focusing process. Having a faith statement also makes it easier to write a purpose statement. A faith statement describes the broadest and most fundamental goal for a sermon. Faith statements usually embody general terms and are easy to write. The faith statement "puts you in the ballpark," so to speak. The following formula sentence works well for writing a faith statement:

THE FAITH STATEMENT

That the people of _____(name of church) be a people who _____

_____

In this statement you say what you want the people to do. Perhaps you desire the people to pray, to trust in God, or to do acts of kindness. For example, if the text illuminates the subject of God's love, your faith statement might read:

THAT THE PEOPLE OF CALVARY BE A PEOPLE WHO BELIEVE THAT GOD LOVES THEM.

This example illustrates the very general nature of faith statements. The more specific purpose statement will relate closely to the faith statement and will grow out of this fundamental goal for the sermon. Working from the general to the specific develops the sermon's purpose in a logical and systematic way. You should write a faith statement for each sermon. Remember that writing faith statements comes easily and should not take much time.

WRITING A PURPOSE STATEMENT

The purpose statement describes in one or two sentences the sermon's exact purpose. In his book, *How to Design and Deliver a Speech*, Leon Fletcher uses a formula for writing purpose statements that works well (152). When we follow Fletcher's guidelines, writing clear and focused purpose statements becomes much easier. He suggests following three basic principles.

A PURPOSE STATEMENT MUST BE

1. Worded with the congregation in mind.
2. Worded in exact, specific, and precise terms.
3. Worded as an attainable, reasonable, and practical goal for the sermon.

PRINCIPLE # 1 - WORDED WITH THE CONGREGATION IN MIND.

We want sermons to have an effect upon a specific congregation. For this reason, the purpose of the sermon must focus on that congregation. Speech teachers call this "the audience principle." This means that when preparing a sermon, you keep your congregation at the center of your thinking. They are the people you desire to affect. Your purpose statement focuses on what you want the congregation to do, think, believe, or value after they have heard the sermon. For example, it would not work to have a purpose statement such as:

THE PURPOSE OF MY SERMON IS TO TELL ABOUT JESUS AND HIS LOVE.

If this were your purpose, the sermon would be successful even if no one listened. The preacher simply intends "to tell." His listeners are not asked or challenged to do anything. A sermon purpose statement that uses the words "to tell" describes what the **preacher** does, not the **congregation**. The emphasis should center on what the preacher wants the **congregation** to do.

A purpose statement worded from the congregation's point of view might read as follows:

AFTER THIS SERMON THE CONGREGATION WILL KNOW THE LOVE THAT JESUS HAS FOR THEM.

It may seem like a subtle difference, but it changes everything. The purpose now focuses on the congregation. This forces the preacher to think more about both the audience and the message being delivered. You can write a purpose statement with the congregation in mind if you always begin with the words:

AFTER THIS SERMON THE CONGREGATION WILL......

I can't emphasize enough the importance of using these exact words to begin your purpose statement. The minute you stray from using these words you risk moving the focus away from the congregation.

Principle # 2 - WORDED IN EXACT, SPECIFIC, AND PRECISE TERMS

The second key to writing a well-focused purpose statement involves writing it in specific terms. The more specific a purpose statement is, the more it will help you write and deliver the sermon.

Being specific about theological and religious thought challenges preachers greatly. Other subjects are easier. For example, if an engineer gives a talk on how a hydrogen engine works, his purpose statement almost writes itself. It would read, "After this talk the audience will know how a hydrogen engine works." Armed with this clear and specific purpose statement, a knowledgeable engineer could write this talk in short order.

For preachers, being specific presents a greater challenge. This means you must work harder at it. Writing a well-focused sermon begins by writing a specific purpose statement. Here again Fletcher's formula sentence helps. Beginning each purpose statement with this sentence will guide you into being more specific. How this works will become clear after learning the technique outlined later in this chapter.

PRINCIPLE # 3 - WORDED AS AN ATTAINABLE, REASONABLE, AND PRACTICAL GOAL FOR THE SERMON

Even if you write a specific purpose statement with the congregation in mind, it will still be ineffective if you ask your listeners to do something unattainable. For this reason you should always consider the capabilities of your hearers.

For example, when preaching to children you are limited in what you can expect, so you adjust your purpose accordingly. When speaking to adults the same principle holds true. You focus on attainable and reasonable things. This means giving some thought to your audience's: 1. background, 2. biblical literacy, 3. education, 4. interests, 5. life experience, 6. lifestyle, and any other pertinent factors.

When writing a purpose statement for a stewardship sermon you could say: "After this sermon the congregation will begin to tithe." However, a more realistic and attainable goal for the sermon would be: "After this sermon the congregation will consider tithing."

Giving your purpose statement a reasonable goal will make it easier to write. It will also have a more positive effect on your listeners.

A TECHNIQUE FOR WRITING PURPOSE STATEMENTS

Generally a sermon falls into one of three basic categories.

1. To inform
2. To persuade
3. To inspire

Each of these sermon categories uses verbs typical for developing a purpose statement, including those listed below. After becoming familiar with writing purpose statements, each person will develop a personal list of preferred verbs. Here are some sample verbs for each category.

INFORM	**PERSUADE**	**INSPIRE**
(will or will be able to)	(will)	(will or will be)
define	believe	excited
demonstrate	accept	pleased
describe	realize	welcomed
determine	know	amused
discuss	see	energized
document	understand	thrilled
identify	help	support
name	participate	challenged
know	support	transformed
recall	follow	inspired
remember	switch	accept
find	consider	empowered
recognize	offer	
compare	volunteer	
summarize		

THE PURPOSE STATEMENT

You can see how this works by looking at the following formula sentence:

After this sermon the congregation 1._____(*"will or will be able to" for inform; "will" for persuade; "will be or will" for inspire*) 2._____ (selected verb) 3._____

_____

_____

_____

(*In this space you describe what you want the congregation to do, think, believe, or value after they have heard your sermon.*) Let me now explain more precisely what you place in each blank of this purpose statement.

BLANK # 1 - In the first blank you write a form of the word "will." For verbs taken from the inform verb list you insert the words, *"will or will be able to."* For the persuade verb list, just the word *"will"* is inserted. For the inspire verb list use the word *"will be or will."*

BLANK #2 – For the second blank choose a verb from your verb lists depending on the purpose of the sermon. A sermon meant to inform uses verbs such as recall, identify, name, or remember in the purpose statement. A sermon meant to persuade uses verbs such as believe, understand, accept, know, see, or realize. Sermons meant to inspire use verbs such as excited, thrilled, energized, or challenged.

Using these verbs will make the sermon more specific and will help you identify the goal of your sermon. You can easily get in a rut and begin to use the same verbs over and over again. Occasionally it helps to re-check the list or perhaps consult a thesaurus in order to give your purpose statements and your sermons more variety.

BLANK #3 - In this blank you write the sentence or sentences that describe what you desire the congregation to do, think, believe, or value after they have heard your sermon. Your purpose statement can contain more than one sentence. You need only select another verb and continue with a second or a third sentence. One-sentence purpose statements can be excellent, but purpose statements with two or three sentences can also be effective. Remember, if your purpose statement includes too many sentences you risk not being specific enough. Now, let's take another look at the earlier example of a well-written purpose statement.

AFTER THIS SERMON THE CONGREGATION (1) WILL (2) KNOW (3) THE LOVE THAT JESUS HAS FOR THEM.

Notice that the key verb "know" comes from the inform verb list, so you use the word "will" in the first blank. Then you name what you want the congregation to know after they have heard your sermon. Other verbs could have served for this purpose statement, but each of them would send the sermon in a different direction. Everything depends on the

Process #1 - Purpose

particular idea you want to focus on. For example, if you use the word "remember" from the inform list of verbs, your purpose statement would read:

AFTER THIS SERMON THE CONGREGATION (1) WILL (2) REMEMBER (3) THE LOVE THAT JESUS HAS FOR THEM.

Using the word "remember" calls to mind a very different focus for the sermon. This focus would change even more dramatically if words such as "recognize" or "discuss" or "define" were used. For example, let us consider the word define. You could use this word if you wanted the congregation to learn a special definition of Christ's love. Your purpose statement might read:

AFTER THIS SERMON THE CONGREGATION (1) WILL BE ABLE TO (2) DEFINE (3) THE MEANING OF CHRISTIAN LOVE.

No matter what you choose as your focus, you will find verbs that fit your purpose.

Now, it may seem that such a simple and basic exercise as filling in a few blanks could hardly be worthwhile. However, writing a clear and focused purpose statement will make your sermon more effective and easier to prepare. It will surprise you to learn what a well-written purpose statement does for a sermon. The pastor who takes the time at the beginning of the preaching process to write a clear purpose statement will find it much easier to preach in the extemporaneous mode.

FAITH AND PURPOSE STATEMENT EXAMPLES

Here are some purpose statements I wrote for sermons on various texts and Sundays of the church year:

Trinity Sunday:

Faith Statement: That the people of Calvary be Trinitarian Christians.

Purpose Statement: After this sermon the congregation will understand why it is that we believe in and teach the doctrine of the Trinity.

3rd Sunday after Pentecost:

Faith Statement: That the people of Calvary be a people who witness to their faith.

Purpose Statement: After this sermon the congregation will realize that every Christian can and should witness to the Gospel.

9th Sunday after Pentecost:

Faith Statement: That the people of Calvary be a people who have a positive attitude about the gift of life.

Purpose Statement: After this sermon the congregation will know where to look and how to find the good in this life amidst all of the bad.

Pentecost Sunday:

Faith Statement: That the people of Calvary be a people who know about the power of the Holy Spirit.

Purpose Statement: After this sermon the congregation will realize that the Holy Spirit is a mighty spirit of power who empowers them to do mighty acts.

2ⁿᵈ Sunday in Lent:

Faith Statement: That the people of Calvary be a people who take seriously their call to be a new creation.

Purpose Statement: After this sermon the congregation will not stand on the sidelines with a half-hearted faith; instead they will participate fully in the ministry of the Gospel because they have been born anew from above.

3ʳᵈ Sunday in Lent:

Faith Statement: That the people of Calvary be a people who know that God is accessible.

Purpose Statement: After this sermon the congregation will feel that they have obtained access to God through Jesus Christ, and they will understand what that access means for their lives.

Perhaps as you read these sample purpose statements you thought of things you would include in a sermon on each subject. The purpose statement has a way of getting your creative juices flowing and soon you come up with ideas and approaches to a given text. I have often thought that a web site simply devoted to sample purpose statements would be popular with preachers. Having a purpose in mind when you begin writing a sermon gives you a powerful head start.

When you write a purpose statement it helps to have everything on one page. I have included below a purpose statement formula sheet that will help you do this.

PURPOSE STATEMENT FORMULA SHEET

Date_____Sunday_____
Text_____

FAITH STATEMENT

That the people of _____be a people who (What you want the people to be like)_____

_____

_____

Example: That the people of Calvary be a people who pray.

PURPOSE STATEMENT

After this sermon the congregation (will, will be able to)_____2. (verb) _____

3. (Describe the general topic of your sermon) _____

_____

_____

_____

Example: After this sermon, the congregation 1. will 2. accept 3. the importance of regular daily prayer and seek to find times to pray each day.

Here are a few things to remember when you write purpose statements:

1. You are not restricted to one sentence. For example, you could add the following sentence to the example on the formula sheet. *"and they will understand that the discipline of the Christian life includes prayer."*

2. You can adjust or change your purpose statement during the writing process. Sometimes your sermon takes a different direction from the original purpose. Simply write a new purpose statement and continue.

3. Don't skip this process. Writing a purpose statement is extremely helpful. For example, if you write a good purpose statement for a children's sermon, you almost have the sermon written.

4. Share your purpose statement with other worship planners. I recently had a former student tell me that once he started writing purpose statements he began using them for worship planning. He would write sermon purpose statements several weeks in advance and give them to worship leaders for their planning. He said it helped coordinate the worship service around a single theme.

IN CONCLUSION

This chapter suggests that having a purpose for your sermon will make it easier to write and easier to speak freely. An equally important premise is that people will listen and benefit more from a sermon that has a purpose. In his book, *The Tipping Point,* Malcom Gladwell cites a study made in the 1960's in preparation for putting the children's show Seseme Street on the air. Researchers wanted to know what would hold children's attention long enough for them to learn from a TV program.

They discovered it wasn't the bells and whistles that kept children's attention but rather the story itself. The show's story had to make sense to even the youngest viewer. In her pioneering research on this subject Elizabeth Lorch, a psychologist at Amherst College, made this observation after elaborate testing of the Sesame Street format: "There were predictable influences on what made the children look back at the TV screen, and these were not trivial things, not just flash and dash." Lorch once reedited an episode of Sesame Street so that certain key scenes of some of the sketches were out of order. If kids were only interested in flash and dash, that shouldn't have made a difference. The show, after all, still had songs and Muppets and bright colors and action and all the things that make Sesame Street so wonderful. But it did make a difference. The kids stopped watching. If they couldn't make sense of what they were looking at, they weren't going to watch (101).

If children will watch and learn from a TV program only if it makes sense, it follows that adults will have an easier time listening and learning from a sermon that has a purpose. It has to do with the way people learn and the way they listen. Writing purpose statements will put us on the right track from the beginning of the sermon preparation process. I hope I have convinced you to give it a solid try.

Chapter 7
Process #2 – Writing

Recently I watched the Emmy Awards. I found it particularly interesting when they gave out the awards for television writing. The presenter began by stating how important writers are to television shows. He then quoted a popular saying among actors: "Remember, if it's not on the page, it's not on the stage."

What happened next surprised me. The Emmy for writing in a situation comedy went to 14 writers for the Frasier show. It astounded me that it took 14 writers to write a half-hour situation comedy. Then came the award for best writing in late-night television. The Tonight Show won this award, and at least a dozen writers came up. This surprised me again because so much of this show involves interviewing guests.

I had two thoughts as I watched these awards given to television writers. First, when it comes to preaching, "If it's not in the manuscript, it's not in the pulpit." Second, creative writing must be very difficult if it takes 13 or 14 writers for each television show. I came away with a new appreciation for what pastors do every week when we write an original 15- or 20-minute sermon. I can't think of anyone else in the culture who does this kind of writing on a regular basis except perhaps some newspaper columnists.

Recently the Hollywood writers went on strike. For three months this brought the production of movies and television to a screeching halt. If anyone ever doubted the importance of what writers do in the entertainment industry, that doubt no longer exists. I believe that writing is equally as important in the preparation of sermons.

Pastors who attend my Process Preaching seminars exhibit surprise when they learn that writing is such a central part of the Process Preaching System. This surprise stems from their erroneous belief that extemporaneous preaching, like impromptu preaching, requires little or no preparation. Actually, preparation stands at the center of extemporaneous preaching. This preparation begins with writing a full manuscript.

About the importance of writing in sermon preparation Thomas Long writes: "Some preachers attempt to develop the ability to preach without notes because of the amazed approval often given to this method by congregations, but the oratorical nimbleness of the preacher is a pseudo value in the Christian context. The church finally does not need to experience the presence of the preacher, it needs rather to hear the claims of the Christian faith through the preacher. If the avoidance of written materials causes the content of the sermon to be lost, ultimately all is lost" (184).

The Process Preaching System converts the written word to the oral word. This requires a written manuscript. In a letter I send out to pastors about to take the Process Preaching seminar,

I ask them to bring a sermon manuscript. I remind them that Process Preaching is a course on delivery. If they don't have something to deliver, I can't help them.

This book focuses on sermon delivery, but I do have things to say about writing. Some of these things are common knowledge in the sermon-writing world, while others relate specifically to extemporaneous preaching.

WHY WRITE A FULL MANUSCRIPT?

I strongly suggest writing a full manuscript for these reasons:

A. You create a sermon by writing. During the writing process your sermon takes form. Everything you discover during your preparation and research comes together when you write.

B. Writing a sermon manuscript increases your focus. If you don't write it down, you might forget what you planned to say. Speaking freely without a written text often leads to rambling and useless repetition.

C. Writing helps you edit and clarify what goes into your sermon. Many pastors fear that speaking freely will cause them to say inappropriate things. By writing out your sermon in full and then orally rehearsing it, you greatly reduce the possibility of saying something you shouldn't. In twenty-five years of preaching extemporaneously, I have never said something from the pulpit I did not plan to say.

Saying the wrong thing in a sermon can be devastating. I have a colleague who preaches in an impromptu manner. He once swore in a sermon, greatly upsetting the congregation. He was fortunate to keep his job.

D. With a written manuscript you can control the length of a sermon. Most preaching situations have rigid time restraints. After a little practice you will know approximately how long it takes to preach a four- or five-page manuscript extemporaneously.

E. Writing a sermon manuscript gets the brain working. As the writing takes place, many ideas emerge. When we write we literally give birth to our sermon.

F. Having a hard copy of your sermon provides many benefits.

1. You need a manuscript during the oral rehearsal / run-through process.
2. It helps you when you deliver your sermon. Although you will not read word for word what you have written, the manuscript guides your delivery.
3. If you have a memory lapse, your manuscript can save you. You will find this particularly helpful when you first begin to preach extemporaneously.
4. Sometimes parishioners request a copy of a sermon.
5. You may wish to save the text for later use.

SOME SUGGESTIONS FOR SERMON WRITING

During the course of a career in writing sermons, each pastor develops a personal way of doing things. However, many "tricks of the trade" can help one's writing. Here are three helpful ideas that relate specifically to the Process Preaching System.

1. Using a computer

The computer did to the typewriter what the chain saw did to the ax – it rendered it obsolete. In the Process Preaching System, a word processor can help. During the writing process, you can easily add things or make changes. Then, following the oral rehearsals, you can re-write or re-arrange the manuscript if necessary. The computer helps out psychologically as well. You will make necessary changes because you can do them so easily. Before word processors, we tended to say, "what I have written, I have written."

2. Writing extemporaneously

In an extemp delivery you do not say exactly what you wrote. You convert your written words to oral language. This means you do not have to carefully craft every sentence. Although the writing needs to be good, you spend much less time editing. You still use your best language and writing skills, but don't need to have things perfect. If at a later time you wish to publish your sermon, you can edit the manuscript and adapt your words for a reading audience.

In writing this book I have edited and revised every sentence, paragraph, and page at least ten times, mainly for clarity and economy. Sermons or speeches read word for word also require this kind of editing.

However, for an extemporaneous delivery, elaborate editing is not necessary. Once you have written what you intend to say, move on to the next thing. Remember for your final delivery, you will not use the exact words and phrases you have written. If, in the past, you have been carefully crafting every sentence of your manuscript, you can now use this time for oral rehearsal.

3. Leave some open spaces

In order to facilitate the delivery process, leave some empty spaces on the manuscript. Hit the space bar and the enter key often. During the delivery process you will find it easier to follow a manuscript not all crowded together like the page of a book.

PREACHING FROM A MANUSCRIPT OR FROM NOTES

Some homileticians recommend preaching from an outline of your manuscript. In the Process Preaching System, you need no outline because you use your full manuscript to guide your delivery. Here are a few reasons why:

A. When you do your run-throughs, you want to know exactly what you plan to say. If you use only sketchy notes you can easily forget what they refer to. With a manuscript you know exactly what you intended to say.

B. By using your manuscript as a guide for delivery, you eliminate the time-consuming step of writing an outline or notes.

C. In the Process Preaching System you use your manuscript during the oral rehearsals. You should use this same document for the actual preaching. After you orally rehearse a sermon, you will remember where things are located on each page. Introducing a different document (i.e. an outline) at the time of delivery may confuse you.

D. I once tried to preach freely from notes and filed these notes with my old sermon manuscripts. Several years later I came across these notes and noticed that when I read them I had no idea what they referred to. On the other hand, old sermon manuscripts can be referenced and used in many different ways.

PRELIMINARY WORK / THE FLOW CHART.

In extemporaneous preaching it helps if your sermon follows a logical pattern. The brain remembers things better if they make good sense and if the thoughts of the sermon flow naturally. Without a logical pattern to follow, the brain gets stuck and can't continue. The brain actually stops you and says "You can't go there, it doesn't make any sense."

The brain will stop you less often if you do some preliminary organizing of material. To help with this organization I use a sermon "Flow Chart." This chart serves as a guide for writing the sermon. I have included a copy of this flow chart on the following page that you can print for your use. In order to have plenty of room to write, I recommend scaling the chart up to fit and print on an 11" x 17" sheet of paper.

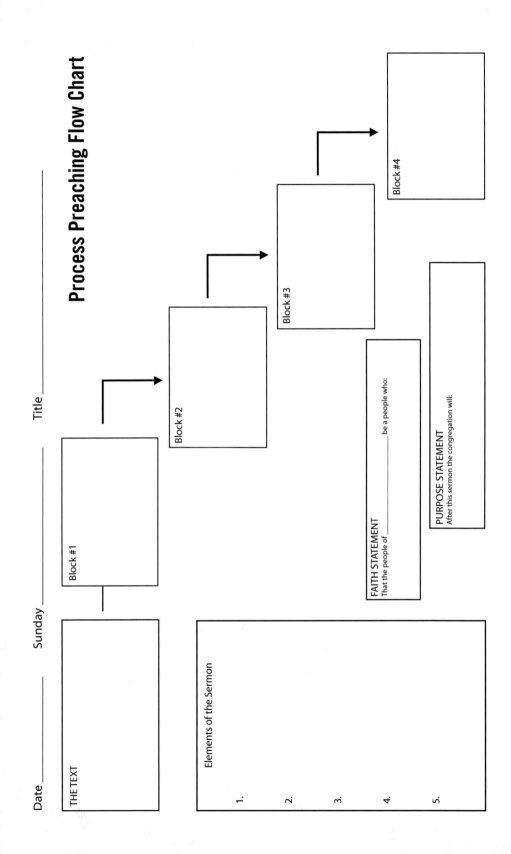

Process Preaching Flow Chart

Date _____ Sunday _____ Title _____

THE TEXT

Block #1

Block #2

Block #3

Block #4

Elements of the Sermon

1.

2.

3.

4.

5.

FAITH STATEMENT
That the people of _____ be a people who:

PURPOSE STATEMENT
After this sermon the congregation will:

I once served a congregation that decided to hire an architect to help them design an addition to the church. At our first meeting the architect quizzed us about how the space would be used. He asked about the purpose of the project, who would be using the space, and what kinds of meetings or events would take place there. The architect took elaborate notes, and then asked if he could talk to people from each group using the space. After he completed his research, he wrote a summary of the information gathered. He then drew a sketch or preliminary design for the building.

A flow chart is like an architect's preliminary design, only for a sermon. After all of your research and information gathering, you use the flow chart to sketch out a preliminary design. This sketch becomes your guide as you write your manuscript. Here are some suggestions for using the sermon flow chart.

A. Faith and purpose statements

To begin using the Flow Chart, transfer your Faith and Purpose Statements onto the Flow Chart. Since these statements describe the goal of the sermon, you should refer to them often in the writing process. They will help you make decisions about what to include in your sermon and will help you focus on a single purpose. By referring to these statements often during the writing process, you can tell what to include and what to leave out.

B. The Biblical text

In this box, you write down the textual reference or the portion of the text you will focus on in your sermon.

C. Title

I always recommend writing a title for your sermon. It gives you another opportunity to express your sermon's purpose. It also alerts the congregation to the sermon's topic. This allows them to start thinking about the subject before the service begins and become better listeners.

D. Elements of the sermon

In this space, you list items you plan to include in your sermon: the stories, illustrations, theological points, or special references that have emerged during your brainstorming and exegesis. The selection process for what you will include in your sermon begins here. During the exegetical and brainstorming work, no doubt you took notes. Now select those items that fit the sermon's purpose. Transfer these items to the list of elements on the flow chart.

E. Sermon blocks

In this step, arrange and combine selected elements to form the various sections of the sermon. These sections become blocks on the flow chart. In his book *Preaching for the People*, Lowell Erdahl calls them chunks of thought. He has some great suggestions for laying them out (79). Whatever you call these blocks they become the major parts of the sermon.

For example, the first block of your sermon may be an illustration or a re-telling of the text. Choosing the block that begins the sermon, the blocks that follow, and the order of the blocks will take some thought. Later, as you write the sermon, you may want to change the order. Then, in the delivery process, you may re-arrange these blocks again. The Process Preaching System allows you to do this easily.

You can have any number of blocks in a sermon. Having more than four or five blocks, however, might obscure your purpose or disrupt the flow of the sermon. I have a friend who regularly has ten or twelve blocks in his sermon and it works well for him.

You are now ready to begin writing your sermon. Filling in a flow chart makes writing much easier. It will give you an excellent guide to follow. You will discover that carefully preparing a flow chart rewards your effort. In fact, every minute you spend developing a flow chart will take at least one minute off your writing time.

In addition, I suggest placing both the faith statement and the purpose statement at the top of your first page. It also helps to print a copy of these statements and tape them above your computer screen for ease of access. With this preliminary work completed, you can begin writing a manuscript for your extemporaneous sermon.

SOME FINAL COMMENTS ON WRITING.

A. I agree with Michael Rogness who writes: "The obvious solution to avoid reading sermons is the worst solution: Not write the sermon out at all. There are occasions when we may not have time to write a sermon out in full, but those should be rare. For long-term growth and improvement in preaching there is no substitute for careful preparation of a manuscript. Pastors who skimp on writing inevitably skimp on preparation. Despite whatever native ability they may have, they soon become shallow and trite in the pulpit. The challenge is to prepare the sermon well, then deliver it well" (96).

B. During my 40-year career in the parish, I was always amazed each time I wrote a sermon. The fact that I came up with something new every week also surprised me. Sometimes I looked at the texts for a given Sunday and drew a complete blank. Then I would start digging into a particular text, and by Friday I would come up with enough material for a sermon.

Writing a sermon every week helped me see how powerfully the Holy Spirit works in the lives of preachers. When I took enough time to work on a sermon, the inspiration would always come. Like so many things in life, preaching seems to rely on the close connection between inspiration and perspiration. If you set aside several hours each week to write a sermon and then spend that time diligently, you will come up with something. The power of the Holy Spirit will produce this little miracle in you every week you proclaim the Gospel.

Martin Luther understood well the difficulty pastors face
in writing sermons. Luther summed it up when he wrote:
"Preparing sermons is hard mental and spiritual work, little
appreciated by people who don't do it. Sure it would be hard for
me to sit, 'in the saddle.' But then again I would like to see the
horseman who could sit still for a whole day and gaze at a book
without worrying or dreaming or thinking about anything else.
Ask a Cantzelkshriber, a preacher or speaker, how much work
it is to speak and preach. The pen is very light, that is true. But
in this work the best part of the human body (the head), the
noblest member (the tongue) and the highest work (speech)
bear the brunt of the load and work the hardest, while in other
kinds of work either the hand, the foot, the back or other
members do the work alone so the person can sing happily
or make jokes freely, which a sermon writer cannot do. Three
fingers do it all (the work of writing) but the whole body and
soul have to work" (Meuser 44).

During the summers of my college and seminary career I
literally dug ditches. I worked for a road building company as
a common laborer. I can't remember a time when I was more
relaxed and at ease than those summer days. Luther rightly
points out that such a state of mind would not be possible
when we write and when we preach. In writing and preaching
the whole body and soul are called upon to work.

C. Pastors do a lot of writing such as newsletter articles, columns for local newspapers, letters of comfort and encouragement. This means that pastors have daily opportunities to hone their writing skills. These are the same writing skills they use for writing sermons.

Putting time and energy into writing a sermon manuscript remains an important and extremely valuable part of sermon preparation. A second preparation is now necessary – oral rehearsal. Now that you have a written document to follow, you are ready to begin the third process in the Process Preaching System—Delivery.

Chapter 8
Process #3 - Delivery

The third and final process in the Process Preaching System is delivery. This final process centers on oral rehearsal. During the oral rehearsal of your sermon, the process of converting the written word (the manuscript) to the oral word (what you actually say) takes place. Oral rehearsal sets extemporaneous preaching apart from other modes of delivery. The Process Preaching System gives you a workable method for doing these oral rehearsals. By using this method for 60 to 90 minutes the preacher can prepare a 15- or 20- minute sermon for extemporaneous delivery.

I call these oral rehearsals "run-throughs." Running through each block or section of a sermon several times enables the preacher to break away from the written text and preach freely. During these run-throughs, what you have written takes on its oral life. The goal of these run-throughs is to preach the sermon freely. When you complete the run-through process, you will not have your sermon memorized, but you will remember it. Perhaps this sounds a little confusing right now. It will make better sense once you have followed the steps outlined below.

The idea of doing oral rehearsals may be difficult for us to accept. As Thomas Long suggests, it may even go against our better judgment. "Should sermons be rehearsed aloud? That question never fails to provoke a squirm of embarrassment among preachers, since the language of rehearsal smacks of performance and play-acting. If we know the content of our sermon and believe what we are going to say in the sermon, why should we practice it? Would it not be more authentic simply to stand up and preach it "for real" the first time?" (186). Later, Long makes it clear that he considers oral rehearsal essential to sermon preparation.

In order to preach extemporaneously, you must rehearse your sermon. Perhaps knowing why you do it will help you willingly rehearse. You do not rehearse your sermon in order to perform it better. Musical numbers are performed, plays are performed; musicians and actors put long hours into rehearsal so that they can perform better. Sermons, however, are not performances. Sermons are attempts to communicate the Gospel good news. You rehearse your sermon not to *perform* it better, but rather to *communicate* it better. The message takes center stage, and rehearsal makes it possible to preach that message in a clear and powerful way.

Extemporaneous preaching requires a particular kind of oral rehearsal. In fact, Process Preaching grew out of the discovery that by running through a sermon in a particular way, a preacher can speak freely in the extemporaneous mode.

A METHOD FOR DOING ORAL REHEARSALS.

In this chapter I outline a method for doing oral rehearsals. Mastering this method will make it possible for you to preach extemporaneously. I have included with this book a DVD recording in which I demonstrate how these oral rehearsals look and sound in real life. After reading this chapter and watching the video, you should be able to do the oral rehearsals necessary to preach your sermon freely.

Remember, these are "oral" rehearsals. This means that you speak the sermon out loud. Running through the sermon in your mind or sub-verbalizing the sermon does not work for this process. For some reason, when you speak the sermon out loud, the brain does its best job of converting the written word to the oral word and remembering it at the same time. It may seem awkward at first to rehearse your sermon out loud. In the end, however, it will amaze you how natural it feels and how easily the words come to you.

STEP ONE – CHOOSING A TIME FOR DOING THE RUN-THROUGHS.

The closer to the time of delivery you do your run-throughs the better. You will be using a type of memory that only lasts about 24 hours. The best time to do your run-throughs is right before you preach. You can also do your run-throughs the day or evening before you preach. Rehearsing your sermon any earlier risks not remembering things very well.

You forget much of your sermon after 24 hours because of something known as transience. Transience causes the brain to forget and thereby make room for new information. Most pastors have experienced transience when a parishioner tells them on Wednesday how much they appreciated last Sunday's sermon. Usually, when this happens the pastor has to think hard in order to remember the sermon. Transience actually helps us because we don't want last week's sermon still in our memory as we work on a new one.

For approximately 24 hours after we do our run-throughs the sermon will remain fresh and strong in our minds. If we wait any longer, we will forget much of what we learned. This makes choosing and setting aside a time close to the time of delivery very important.

STEP TWO – CHOOSING A LOCATION FOR DOING THE RUN-THROUGHS

Choose a good location for running through your sermon. If possible, run through your sermon in the sanctuary or hall where it will be preached. If this room is unavailable, choose a setting similar to it. If your church has a chapel, that would be ideal. You could also set up a fellowship hall or other large room to simulate the setting of the sanctuary. Being in a setting that approximates where you normally preach helps you imagine the presence of the congregation. Visualizing things in this way actually helps your mind produce the words and phrases you use in your delivery.

You can do your oral rehearsals in many other locations. Pastors have shared several with me over the years:

1. I have a friend who has a long commute and does some oral rehearsing in his car. Of course this can be distracting, especially when trying to follow a manuscript. It might work well, however, for going over stories or illustrations. You could also use this time to run through things like retelling the text.

2. One of my students wrote that she did her run-throughs on Saturday evening as she walked around the park. She brings her manuscript with her, and before long her arms are flailing as she gets completely into her sermon.

3. I know pastors who run through their sermons while sitting at their desk or standing up and walking around their office.

4. Since retiring I have preached in several unfamiliar settings and have had to do my run-throughs at home. Sometimes I set up a music stand in the basement and do my run-throughs there. I have also done them sitting in my office chair with a music stand by my side.

There are endless possible locations for doing your run-throughs. However, it still holds true that the closer you approximate the setting in which you preach, the better. For some reason your creative juices flow more freely when you have your audience in mind. Rehearsing in the right setting helps this happen.

The two most important things to keep in mind when choosing a time and a location for your run-throughs are:

    a. Allow ample time.

    b. Have complete privacy.

Setting ample time aside will allow you to avoid rushing things or quitting too early. At the same time, running through your sermon in private makes it possible to be completely relaxed. The likelihood of your experimenting or trying different ways of saying things is greatly enhanced by being unhurried and in a private setting.

During the course of the Process Preaching seminar I demonstrate how oral rehearsals are done. I feel rather foolish and vulnerable struggling through an oral rehearsal in front of a group of pastors. Because of this I dread doing it. However, my demonstrations are always appreciated and are a necessary part of teaching pastors how to do oral rehearsals. You, on the other hand, have the privilege of rehearsing in complete privacy.

Parishioners have difficulty understanding the need or purpose of rehearsing sermons. Many believe that preachers are naturally gifted and can preach freely without practice. These same people when attending a piano concert, expect the pianist to be fully rehearsed. Still, they think it unusual that a preacher needs rehearsal to deliver a sermon.

STEP THREE – DOING THE RUN-THROUGHS

After you have selected a time and a place for doing your run-throughs, the actual run-through process can begin. In this step I will explain how to go about it.

A. Re-focus

Before beginning your run-throughs, you should review your faith and purpose statements. You do this to assess what you hope to accomplish in your sermon. Here again it helps to speak your purpose out loud. When I do this I step down into the imaginary congregation and explain what I will preach about. I might say, "Today I want to talk to you about prayer. Prayer is central to our Christian faith and one of the great resources we have for both strengthening and growing our faith." I might continue with even more of an explanation. Remember, having your purpose well in mind will assist you as you begin to speak your sermon freely. Running through this explanation before actually beginning your run-throughs will focus your purpose clearly in your mind.

During my years in the parish, I set Fridays aside for writing my sermon. Sunday morning on my way to church I would start thinking about my sermon and often could remember very little about it. It never worried me, however, because I knew that in an hour or two of oral rehearsal I would have my sermon ready to deliver freely.

B. Block by Block

After re-focusing on the purpose of your sermon, you now run through your sermon one block at a time. You run through each block or section until you have it down pat. You then move on to the next block of your sermon. Once you have all the blocks prepared you are ready to preach the sermon.

You begin the actual rehearsal process by reading the first block of your sermon silently to yourself. You may think that reading your sermon out loud will help you preach it extemporaneously. Actually, you could read your sermon out loud 100 times and fail to preach it freely. Also, there would be no difference between what you say during the first reading and the 100th reading. Communication improves very little by reading a script over and over again. Your brain can actually rest when you read, and you will make no progress in the direction of speaking freely.

Recently I watched a television blooper show re-playing some classic huge mistakes made on live television. I was surprised to see that people reading rather than people speaking freely made the most bloopers. This happens because when we read our brains can remain disconnected from what we say. One of the newscasters remained so disconnected from what he read that even after making a huge mistake he kept reading as if nothing had happened. If he had been speaking freely this probably wouldn't have happened. His brain and his words would be too closely connected.

After reading the first block of your sermon through a few times to yourself, turn away from the manuscript and try to say what you have written freely. Position the manuscript in such a way that when you turn away you cannot see it. If the words are in front of your eyes, you will be tempted to look down and read what you have written. If you stand during your run-throughs, simply step aside from the pulpit or lectern to speak. If sitting, you can place your manuscript on a music stand off to your side.

When you preach the sermon, return to having your manuscript directly in front of you. For now, however, keep it off to your side. Once you step aside or look away from your manuscript and try to freely express the thoughts that you have written, your brain will find new and often better words for the same thoughts. The words will change but the meaning will remain the same. In order to move towards preaching extemporaneously, you must look away from the manuscript and try to speak freely.

When you try to say the first sentences of your manuscript, you might use the exact words that are on the page. However, before you get very far, you won't remember exactly what you wrote. Now you will be forced to move away from the exact words of your text. You will begin to express the meaning of what you have written in words that come to mind at the moment of utterance.

Normally you will only get a little way into your sermon during this first run-through. If you begin with an illustration or the retelling of the text, you might get a little further. Typically you will get stuck almost immediately and be unable to say much of what you have written. Once you get stuck, look again at what you have written. This time circle or underline key words. If you have a list of things in this block, you can put numbers by them and other marks to help you remember them.

Now turn or step away from your manuscript once again and try to say what you have written. This time you may get a little further into the text. Once again return to your manuscript to see what you have written. You may discover more phrases or key words that you forgot during your first or second run-through. Mark these words and turn away again to try to say what you have written.

Usually during this third run-through you suddenly can say what you have written. You won't be using the same words, but the meaning of what you have written will remain. A small miracle takes place during this third run-through. For some reason the brain needs three tries to figure out and remember what you intend to say. Once your brain understands what you are trying to say, it converts the written word to an oral word and stores it in your memory. Don't try to memorize what you have written word for word or try to say things exactly as written. Remember, you used written language when you wrote the manuscript, and now you want to use oral language.

Something that helps make speaking freely possible is the fact that there are many ways of saying the same thing. This gives you the freedom to use different words without changing the meaning.

Recently we had a cold month of July here in Minnesota and we broke several records. One evening the weather reporter said, "Today we established a new low high for this day." This was a rare occurrence since the previous record went back to 1939. My wife and I talked about this and found ourselves describing it very differently. Later I wrote down several ways we found to express this same event.

1. Today was a record low high temperature for this date.

2. Today we achieved a new low high temperature.

3. Today the high temperature was the lowest it has ever been for this date.

4. Today's high temperature was the lowest ever for this day.

5. The high temperature today was the lowest high ever recorded on this day.

6. Today the high temperature did not get above the lowest high temperature ever recorded on this day.

There are certainly many other ways of expressing this same thought. Some work better for a written presentation while others work well in an oral setting. Realizing this will help you relax during the run-through process as you find yourself changing things slightly during each subsequent run-through.

During my seminars I work with students individually on this run-through process. Recently one of my students was having difficulty getting more than a few words into her sermon before she needed to look down to see what came next. Even after three or four run-throughs she was only getting into her sermon a sentence or two. She was trying to share a story from a mission trip she recently attended. I told her to simply tell me the story as if she were telling it to her best friend. She looked a little puzzled but then started telling me her incredible story. She had no problem getting through the entire story. Earlier she tried to memorize what she had written instead of telling the story freely. If you have difficulty getting very far into the first section of your sermon after three or four run-throughs, you may be trying to memorize your text instead of speaking it freely.

Every time you run through a block of your sermon, it should come out a little differently. If it does, you know you are speaking freely and not memorizing the text. Your final presentation will combine all of your run-throughs with whatever you come up with at the moment of delivery.

During the first two run-throughs you cannot imagine being able to speak freely what you have written. During this time you may stumble along and feel panic setting in. Even after using this method for the past 20 years, I still have days when I don't think this system will work. I make little progress during the first couple run-throughs. I start thinking that although this method has worked in every sermon I have preached for the past 20 years, it won't work this time.

If this happens to you, simply take a look at your watch and say to yourself, "I am going to run through this block for 15

minutes, and if after that time I am still stuck, I will give up."
If you do this, you will never have to give up. As long as you
put in the time required you will eventually speak your sermon
freely. Your brain might change things around a little, but you
will eventually succeed.

Unfortunately, many pastors who have tried to speak
extemporaneously have given up after the first or second run-
through. They become frustrated when they fail to get very
far. This makes them think they will never be able to speak
their sermons freely. If they could make it to the third or
fourth run-through, they would discover that they can preach
extemporaneously just fine. It is unrealistic to expect your brain
to convert your written word to an oral word during the first
run-through. By running through each section three or four
times you give your brain the opportunity it needs to do both
the converting and the remembering needed for the moment of
delivery.

C. Continuing

Once you master the first block of your sermon, you go on
to the next block. A block might be anything from a short
paragraph to an entire page. For example, if you begin with a
story or retelling of the text, this might fill an entire page on
your manuscript. On the other hand, if your first block simply
introduces your sermon, it might take only a few sentences.

Remember, you run through each block separately, so you
don't need to go through the first block again until the time of

delivery. However, during your final run-through of the second block you should go back and pick up the last sentence or two of the first block. You do this in order to practice transitioning into this second section of your sermon. Do this after each block of your sermon. Transitions are very important, so you need to run through these movements between sections.

It may seem odd that you do not run through your entire sermon from start to finish during your oral rehearsals. Remember, once you have completed running through a block, you are ready to speak that section freely. This means that to deliver the entire sermon you need only know the order of the blocks. If you have your manuscript in front of you, you have ready access to this information. Listeners are not distracted if you look at your manuscript to see what comes next. People expect preachers to have notes or a manuscript in front of them. You will communicate well as long as, after checking your manuscript, you come back to the people and preach freely.

Extemporaneous preaching does not mean preaching without manuscript or notes. Rather, it means preaching without reading your manuscript. Preaching without notes does not by itself make for effective communication. Speaking extemporaneously, however, dramatically increases the level of communication. If you remember this, you will understand more clearly the purpose of your manuscript and how to use it.

In public speaking, fluency is highly overrated. I indicated earlier that when you preach freely your delivery will include starts and stops, ah's and um's, backtracking and repetition. Similarly, checking your manuscript to see what comes next will also make your preaching less fluent. These moments of silence may seem like an eternity to you. However, your listeners will find them perfectly normal. Listeners actually appreciate these pauses and use them to catch up and process what they have heard. It may take awhile getting used to this lack of smoothness and fluency. Once you realize how it often aids communication, you will stop worrying about it.

D. Concluding

The conclusion of your sermon needs special attention. As you approach the end, you should note exactly where the conclusion begins. You should preach this section without looking at your notes. This extra effort at the end is always worth it. You want to look directly at the congregation and really connect with them during the conclusion.

You may tend to neglect the conclusion. It comes at the end of the run-through process when you are getting weary. Fortunately, at the actual time of delivery this part of the sermon seems to come easily. In fact, it often takes on a life of its own. Changes to the conclusion often occur at the moment of delivery. Nevertheless, do not rely completely upon the inspiration of the moment. Always work hard on your conclusion.

STEP FOUR – IN ADDITION

Here are a few more things that come into play during the run-through process and some suggestions for dealing with them.

DISCOVERIES

During the run-through process, you will discover many things about your sermon. You will see where your sermon makes good sense and where it doesn't. You will think of things to add, both large and small, and you will often rearrange the blocks. This happens because your brain sorts things out for you during the run-through process. Sermons need to make good sense if you want to speak them freely. For this reason, you make changes where your sermon needs adjustments. Here are some suggestions for how to handle these changes:

1. Rearranging

You may discover that the order of things in your sermon requires rearranging. When this happens, you can usually cut and paste your manuscript without rewriting it. If what you rearrange appears on the same page, you can simply mark it to indicate the switch. If you use a word processor and have the time, you can make the changes and then print a new copy.

If you print a new copy, make sure that you use this new version for your final run-throughs and for your delivery. After a couple of run-throughs, you will remember where certain things are on the page. If you change their location by reprinting and do not run through this new version, you will have a hard time finding things during your delivery. Amazingly, your brain will look for something at the top of the page if it was located there during your run-throughs. If you use the final edition of your sermon for your run-throughs, you will have no problem.

2. Adding things

During the run-through process you may discover items you wish to add to your sermon. Perhaps you have discovered a word, a phrase, or even an additional illustration that you particularly like. When this happens, simply write these things into the spaces and margins of your manuscript.

Each time you run through a block of your sermon, you will change the way you say things. Do not write down the ordinary changes in language that take place as your brain converts your written manuscript to an oral presentation. Write down only the important additions, those things not included in your original manuscript. You could waste much time writing notes on your manuscript if you mark down minor changes in language.

Write your additions down so that you can run through them and incorporate them into your sermon. As long as these notes serve as an adequate guide for your run-throughs, you do not have to rewrite and reprint your manuscript with all of your additions and corrections. In fact, it helps not to. The marks you make on your manuscript give you important guideposts during delivery. If you reprint your manuscript, it may look nice and neat, but it will lose some important guideposts that are already firmly etched in your brain.

3. Direct quotations

When a sermon includes direct quotations such as scripture passages or poetry, you need not memorize them. Instead, simply print them out in bold or all capitals and read them out loud. If you want to memorize something you certainly can. However, taking time to memorize direct quotations usually doesn't reward the time and effort. In fact, when you read something out loud in the middle of a sermon, it can provide your listeners a nice break or refreshing change.

Several things are important to remember when you read things out loud.

1. You should always let your listeners know you are going to read to them. You can say something like "as we read in Matthew 14" or "Mark Twain once wrote." You do this because people listen differently when read to than when listening to someone speak freely. Letting them know what's coming enables them to change their listening gears.

2. When reading a quotation don't worry about eye contact. Focus on the text and read it well. Recently I was listening to a person read the lessons on Sunday morning. It seemed like he kept losing his place. When I looked up at him I realized he was pausing at the end of each sentence to make eye contact with the congregation. He had learned that eye contact was important in public speaking, so he often looked up from the text. In truth, when reading quotations fluency trumps eye contact.

3. When you have finished reading a quotation, you should pause briefly and return to speaking freely. Your listeners will

realize, without your telling them, that you have finished the quotation and are back to speaking freely.

MARKING YOUR TEXT

During the run-through process it helps to mark your text. Here are a few reasons for doing this.

1. Marks that you make during your first run-through help you during your subsequent run-throughs.

2. It helps during the final delivery to have things well marked for easy reference when you need it.

3. Marks help your brain picture the sermon and how it unfolds. A well-marked manuscript aids the brain in the remembering process.

You can use colored highlighters for marking your text so that things really stand out, or you can simply use a pen. If you use a pen, you won't have to change marking instruments every time you want to write something into the text.

Some things to highlight on your manuscript are:

1. Key Words – The first thing you should highlight are the key words in each block. When you remember a key word in a sentence or paragraph, it primes your pump and gets you going on the right track. As you run through each block you will discover which words are central to the particular meaning you wish to convey. Once you know and remember key words in a sentence or paragraph, you can preach it more freely.

I am constantly amazed by how the brain uses these key words. You will find that key words can unlock entire files of information stored in your brain. You remember a key word, and suddenly you think of all the other words that surround it. Always underline, highlight, or circle the key words in each block of your manuscript. Then use these words to unlock the storehouse of information available in your memory.

2. **Blocks & Sections** – A second thing to mark on your manuscript are the blocks or sections of your sermon. You can add a series of circled numbers in the margin of the text or put brackets around a section of text to remind you where each block begins and ends. By marking blocks, you both remember and deliver your sermon in sections. As you proceed through your sermon, your eyes move to the places you have marked. You can then see exactly what comes next.

3. **Quotations** – Mark or highlight quotations, key sentences, or ideas in the sermon that you consider to be especially important.

4. **Lists** – When you have a list of things to remember, it helps to number them. The numbers remind you how many things are on the list. If you forget something, you can easily see what you left out.

There are many ways to mark your text. You will come up with your own system once you start doing it on a regular basis.

Here are a few suggestions to get you started:

A. Underline words or phrases
B. Circle words or phrases
C. Number items (good for lists.)
D. Circle the numbers
E. Brackets
F. Roman numerals (good for marking blocks)
G. Box words or phrases
H. A, B, C (also good for lists etc.)
I. Exclamation marks
J. Stars (for key points)
K. Arrows (when things need to be moved)
L. Text notes (simply write your additions and corrections onto the manuscript)

PREACHING WITHOUT NOTES

Sometimes preaching without notes may be desirable or even necessary. I recently had a student from California whose congregation worshiped on the beach every Sunday. There was no pulpit or lectern on which to place his manuscript, and when he tried to use a music stand his notes would often blow away. Naturally he was interested in learning how to preach without notes for these outdoor services.

In my own ministry sometimes I moved away from the pulpit to preach without notes. For example, on Confirmation Sundays, I often came down and stood in front of the class and spoke directly to them. I always did children's sermons without notes, and on communion Sundays I preached from the communion rail without notes.

In the Process Preaching System you can preach without notes by adding two additional steps. First, you memorize the order of the various blocks, and then you run through the sermon start to finish.

In the first step, memorizing the order of things, you once again talk to an imaginary congregation. Instead of going over your entire sermon during this step, you simply deliver an outline. Imagine that you are an orchestra conductor telling an audience about the various parts of a symphony. When conductors do this, they identify the symphony's various movements and often explain what they mean.

You do the same thing with your sermon. You run through the order of the blocks orally. It might sound something like this: "I am going to begin my sermon today with an illustration about the time I was hunting in Montana and became hopelessly lost. Then, I will explain how this relates to our text from the book of Exodus. After that, I will explain how this relates to our lives today. I will conclude by sharing my experience of being spiritually lost and eventually being found by God."

You can put as much detail into this outline as you like. You will discover that because you have run through the various blocks of your sermon and know them well, you need remember only their order. Once you do this, you are ready to preach the entire sermon without notes.

The second step added in order to preach without notes is running through the entire sermon. In this final run-through, you will want to go through the sermon from start to finish without interruption. This will give you confidence and secure the sermon firmly in your memory.

Many people believe that extemporaneous speaking means speaking without notes. More accurately, it means speaking freely. On several occasions in this book I have recommended taking your manuscript into the pulpit to guide your delivery. I believe that following a manuscript is the preferred and easiest way to preach freely. I have found that as long as you speak freely you can check your manuscript often during sermon delivery. Remember it is speaking freely that matters, not whether or not you use notes.

If you wish to leave the pulpit behind, you must consider two important things:

1. Because the pulpit is higher than the pews, the congregation can see you well. This extra height helps when we speak our sermons freely. People can see our facial expression and gestures. Good oral communication relies on people seeing these things. If you do move out of the pulpit, I suggest that you stand on the highest level of the chancel. When I have preached at more informal services, I simply place a music stand to the side of the "stage." Then I can walk around and go back to my notes whenever I need to. It has become popular for some pastors to walk up and down the aisles while delivering

their sermon. When they do, only a few people can see them at one time. This limits one's ability to communicate orally.

2. The congregation needs to hear you well. The pulpit usually has the best microphone for this. If you want to move out of the pulpit, you need to pay attention to how your microphone works as you move around the sanctuary. Often a lavaliere microphone works well only when you are facing one direction. The new microphones that attach to your ear and come right to your mouth probably solve this problem. Be sure to check with members of the congregation to make sure they can hear you. Investing in good public address equipment is a crucial congregational investment.

Preaching in the extemporaneous style gives you many opportunities for trying new things. Keep in mind that for an oral communication to be effective, your audience must see and hear you.

SOME FINAL REFLECTIONS ON THE DELIVERY PROCESS.

A. It is worth it.

At times, preaching can be very discouraging. Trying a new way of delivery will definitely have its up and downs. Martin Luther once wrote: "No message would be more pleasing to my ears than the one deposing me from the office of preaching. I suppose I am so tired of it because of the great ingratitude of the people, but much more because of the intolerable hardships which the devil and the world mete out to me. But the poor souls will not let me rest. Then, too, there is a man whose name is Jesus Christ. He says, no. Him I justly follow as one who has deserved more of me." (quoted in Meuser 33).

Five hundred years ago Martin Luther considered preaching to be the hardest thing pastors did. He also believed that it was the most important thing they did. I believe this still to be true. The Baptist preacher, Theodore Adams, once said: "A pastor is asked to do a great many things, but if he/she can't preach, he/she will never get a chance to do any of them." (quoted in Aycock 130)

When congregations enter the call process, they often ask their members what they consider the most important attributes for their new pastor. Preaching nearly always tops the list. We may wish that it were different. It would be good if the other wonderful things pastors do were held in as high regard. As I grew up my grandparents, parents, and uncles and aunts all referred to their pastor as "the preacher." This is not as prevalent today, since terms such as pastor and reverend have risen in popularity. Few pastors today want to be known only as the preacher. Nevertheless, in the eyes of your congregation, preaching remains central to both your job description and your mission.

B. Assessment

In order to put significant amounts of energy and time into extemporaneous preaching, you need to be convinced of its value. Does preaching freely in the extemporaneous mode actually communicate the gospel better than reading a manuscript? This is an important question and difficult to answer. In a recent Process Preaching seminar, a student asked me if there was any proof that preaching freely communicated better than reading sermons out loud. I could not cite any survey or research results that would prove that using oral skills and language work better in an oral setting. I believe that it does, but I can't actually prove it. This means you will have to discover for yourself whether speaking freely makes a difference in your ability to communicate the Gospel.

You can do this by seeking feedback from your congregation. It is difficult to open yourself to suggestions about preaching. However, if you decide to try extemporaneous preaching, it might be the perfect time to try it. Ask a few people in your congregation to fill out an assessment form. Choose people whose opinions you respect or give an assessment form to members of the church council or mutual ministry team.

You can also receive valid feedback from a video recorder. It can be painful to watch a video of your preaching, but it can help you notice things that you need to change in your delivery. I had an intern who caught on very quickly to speaking freely. When she did, she gestured with every word in the same predictable manner. Since we were recording our services, I asked her to watch a video of her sermon. She saw the problem immediately and quickly corrected it.

Another possibility for assessment can come from listening for reactions from the congregation. Subtle comments or a positive word from a parishioner can be encouraging. If you listen carefully to what people say about your preaching, it may be all you need to know that you are heading in the right direction.

C. Conclusion

In the early days of my ministry I was a solo pastor in a small rural parish. One of the regular Sunday morning worshipers wore a hearing aid. Each Sunday, as I began my sermon, he would reach into his shirt pocket and turn off his hearing aid. Shortly thereafter he would be fast asleep until awakened by the post-sermon hymn. This old saint never gave my sermons much of a chance. I believe that preaching freely instead of reading my sermons would have given me a better chance of keeping him awake.

When my grandchildren stay with us and are ready for bed, they ask me to read them a story or two. They often fall asleep in the process, which is a good thing. However, when we sit around the campfire at the cabin telling stories late into the night, they never fall asleep. I believe that's because speaking freely has a way of grabbing people's attention and keeping it. When we use our oral communication skills and preach our sermons freely, we will keep people awake and we will communicate the Gospel with increasing purpose, passion, and power.

Chapter 9
Memory and Process Preaching

The Process Preaching System works because of how the human memory works. During my years of preaching and working with preachers, I have learned about several characteristics of human memory that relate to preaching freely in the extemporaneous mode.

REMEMBERING VS. MEMORIZING

Sometimes students tell me they can't imagine preaching their manuscripts freely because they can't memorize things well. I tell them they don't have to memorize their sermons to preach them freely. I explain that they will only have to **remember** their sermon – a totally different thing than memorizing it. Memorizing a text word for word takes a long time for anyone without a photographic memory. Remembering the general characteristics of our text so that we can deliver it orally takes much less time.

For example, if you can remember the punch line of a good joke, you could probably reproduce the joke orally with ease. If you want to tell the joke just right, you need only rehearse it a few times. In the case of preaching, during the run-through process you place into your memory everything you need to deliver your sermon. The amount of memory effort needed to remember your sermon during the run-throughs amounts to much less than that required for memorizing a text word for word.

ORGANIZATION AND MEMORY

Modern memory researchers say that the central characteristic of human learning is organization. The British Psychologist Alan Baddeley says, "Organization is important at three levels:

1. organization that already exists in one's long–term memory;
2. organization that can be perceived or generated within the material to be learned; and,
3. organization linking these two, thus allowing the new material to be accessed as and when required" (125).

This organizational principle relates to Process Preaching in three different ways.

1. Writing a purpose statement begins the organization phase of writing a sermon. Without a stated purpose for the sermon, good organization becomes difficult to achieve.
2. The flow chart organizes the sermon's flow so that things logically follow one another. Organizing the sermon into blocks helps you remember the sermon during both the rehearsal and the delivery.
3. Having things well ordered enables us to remember what to say and helps our audience remember what's been said.

As proclaimers of the Gospel we want our listeners to learn something. Most oral presenters intend to inform or even entertain an audience. Preachers, on the other hand, want to teach and inspire. If better organization helps make that happen, we should pay close attention to it.

MEANING AND MEMORY

"Much long-term memory for material presented auditorily involves language, and is probably stored more in terms of its meaning than its sound"(Baddeley 23). These words indicate that applying meaning to things helps us remember them. People who teach memory classes encourage their students to apply meaning to the most mundane information in order to remember it better.

To remember sermons, meaning is key. You can remember what to say next if you know the meaning you want to get across. Having a clear purpose and goal puts meaning at the heart of your sermon. If you have the meaning of a particular block of your sermon firmly in mind, the words needed to express that meaning will come to you easily.

TRANSIENCE / FORGETTING

An important aspect of brain function is transience or forgetting. The brain uses transience to make room for new information continually coming in. Transience becomes especially important in short-term and working memory. In these two types of memory we remember things for as little as a few seconds.

In his book *The Seven Sins of Memory*, Daniel Schacter writes: "Working memory allows you to hold on to small amounts of information for short periods of time, usually a few seconds. However, the system must constantly discard what is no longer needed at the moment, and devote its resources to the temporary storage of incoming information. Unless a special effort is made, such as repeating a sentence over and over again, information is lost from the system almost immediately after it enters....we can protect against transience by making a concerted effort to rehearse information"(28).

Over a century ago, Herman Ebbinghaus discovered that repeating information improves memory of what is repeated (Baddeley 108). Thus, by rehearsing information, we can fight off transience and put things into a longer memory store.

This relates to extemporaneous preaching in two ways. First, it means we should not be surprised when we forget our sermons shortly after we preach them. It also tells us that rehearsal is the key to remembering our sermons. Rehearsal prolongs the length of time we remember things. Memory experts have known this for a long time.

THE 24-HOUR MEMORY

Memory experts have identified different kinds of memory. Among these are working memory, which lasts a few seconds, short-term memory, which lasts a little longer and long-term memory. The kind of memory that enables us to remember our sermons for about 24 hours is a type of long-term memory.

Pastors are not interested in remembering their sermons for long periods of time. It would not be good to have last week's sermon floating around in our brains while we work on a new one. This means that the transient nature of this 24-hour long-term memory actually helps us.

Back in college we used to say that the difference between an A student and a C student was only a matter of a few hours. The A student remembered the answers to the questions until one hour after the test, and the C student remembered the answers only until one hour before. This we said with tongue in cheek, but it may have been close to the truth. In the case of the 24-hour memory we use to speak freely, we have a limited window of opportunity for remembering. Thus our oral rehearsals work best as close as possible to the time of delivery.

LEVELS OF PROCESSING

In 1972 memory researchers Craik and Lockhart published a paper on "levels of processing." They suggested that "the more deeply an item is processed, the better it will be remembered, with information processed in superficial sensory terms giving rise to relatively short-lived traces, and phonological processing producing a somewhat more durable trace, while deep semantic processing produces the most durable learning" (quoted in Baddeley 121-122).

The Process Preaching system combines writing purpose statements, organizing the sermon in blocks, writing a manuscript, and oral rehearsal to create a powerful memory trace. This processed memory trace can then be called upon at the moment of delivery to help us speak freely.

ORAL REHEARSAL AND MEMORY

Closely related to the issue of processing for better retention is oral rehearsal. In the world of deep-memory processing lies something called enactment, or doing something physical in connection with what you want to remember. In 1988 Nilsson and Cohen "reported a number of studies indicating excellent learning following enactment. They argue that this reflects the fact that enactment produces such a rich and discriminable memory trace that the influence of these factors is swamped" (Baddeley 122).

As a type of enactment, oral rehearsal enhances memory. It both physically and mentally puts down a memory trace that you can call upon later. By speaking your sermon out loud, you are more likely to remember your thoughts and successfully speak them freely at the time of delivery.

Orally rehearsing your sermon also means that you *hear* the sermon. Even though you are the one who speaks, the fact that you hear the words and not just read them helps the remembering process. Baddeley says this about the difference between hearing and reading: "An auditory presentation is likely to lead to somewhat better recall than visual. So, if you have just heard a telephone number, you are rather more likely to remember it than if you have just read it" (30).

Recently my wife spent a week in the hospital. Every day she saw the same doctor but could not remember the doctor's name even though she had read it on his name tag several times. Quite by accident she said the name out loud a few times and she never forgot it again. There is a very important connection between hearing something spoken and remembering it.

AMAZING QUICKNESS

It surprises me how quickly your brain works when you speak freely. Recently I noticed this when telling my grandson about the college his mother attended. I wanted to tell him about her college town and brag it up a little. Unfortunately I started out all wrong. I said, "Augustana College is" (I meant to say "Sioux Falls is a great little city"), but in the time it took to say "Augustana College is" my brain figured out a new ending for the sentence that would work just fine. I said fluently "Augustana College is in a great mid-size city, Sioux Falls, South Dakota." Because your brain totally engages with your thoughts when you speak freely, it sorts things out with great quickness.

THE PHONOLOGICAL STORE

Memory researchers have identified a connection between remembering things and human speech. This is called the phonological loop. It consists of two things, an articulatory control process and the phonological store. Baddeley explains how this works: "The phonological loop is assumed to comprise two components, a phonological store that is capable of holding speech-based information, and an articulatory control process based on inner speech. Memory traces within the phonological store are assumed to fade and become un-retrievable after about one and a half to two seconds. The memory trace can however be refreshed by a process of reading off the trace into the articulatory control process, which then feeds it back into the store, the process underlying sub vocal rehearsal. The articulatory control process is also capable of taking written material, converting it into a phonological code, and registering it in the phonological store" (52).

When we rehearse our written manuscript out loud, it may be this phonological loop that helps us convert the written words to oral language during the moment of delivery. Whatever the case, the presence of a phonological store clarifies the unique connection between what we write and what we say during the oral rehearsal process.

The advent of the computer age has led to a great deal of research into human memory and how it works. Scientists and medical researchers study human memory in part because of the increasing instance of memory loss among our aging population. We may never know exactly how memory works, but as we learn more about it, we may understand more clearly how the brain converts written language into dynamic oral communication.

Chapter 10
Process Speaking

The Process Preaching System can work well in many non-preaching situations both within the congregation and outside of it. Pastors are asked to speak for many different occasions. The combination of writing and oral rehearsal that characterizes Process Preaching can benefit communication in many of these circumstances. First, I will suggest some situations within the life of the congregation where Process Speaking works well.

WITHIN THE WORSHIP SERVICE

1. The Children's message – I began my attempts at speaking freely with the children's message. I realized early on that when you teach young children, you can't read to them from a prepared script. Speaking freely enabled me to keep the children's attention.

Don't be tempted to short-change the preparation time for the children's message. I once had an intern who began working on his children's message on his way to worship. He would ad-lib the message, and it never went very well. His message seldom had much of a point, and in turn, very little effect upon the children.

You can use an abbreviated form of the Process Preaching System for the children's message. Writing a purpose statement is especially important. Once you have written it, you can easily write the rest of the message. For example, your purpose statement might read: "After this sermon the children will know that Jesus is with them when they are tempted." Once you have a good purpose statement, it takes little effort to write the entire message. Always write a manuscript for the children's message. It will help keep your message short and to the point.

It helps to use a physical object for the children's message. Physical things help the brain remember. Using an object will help both you and the children remember your sermon. For example, for a sermon on temptation, you could have a very thin stick that breaks easily and a very thick stick that would only break with great difficulty. The thin stick represents the child who might give in to temptation easily. However, if the child stays close to the thick stick, which represents Jesus, he or she can resist temptation. An object lesson such as this makes speaking the children's message freely a very easy matter.

When I began speaking the children's message freely, I received positive feedback from the congregation. I had one of the most highly educated members of the church tell me that in the children's message he had finally found his level of understanding. He may have been kidding, but he said it with what seemed a deep sense of appreciation. Looking back now, I believe that his reaction came because I spoke freely to the children.

2. Announcements – If you have an introduction of the day, a welcoming time, or a time for announcements, you should write these things down. It is easy to forget important announcements unless you write them down. Announcements provide an excellent opportunity for speaking freely. Reading announcements does not work well. Orally rehearsing your announcements will improve your fluency and your effectiveness. Speaking them freely will convey the fact that your announcements are important.

3. Prayers – During my entire ministry I wrote out my Sunday morning prayers word for word and read them during the worship service. My current pastor speaks his prayers freely. Both of these methods have their good points. If you write out your prayers in full you will be sure to include everything you want to pray for. You will also include any special prayer requests that have come from the congregation. On the other hand, if you speak them freely your prayers will seem more heartfelt.

The best possible scenario would include writing out your prayers, running through them three times, and praying them freely. Then they would be extemporaneous prayers and have the best of both the written and oral word.

With all of these worship opportunities for speaking freely the problem quickly becomes finding enough time for the run-throughs. I would suggest the following hierarchy of priorities for speaking freely in a service:

1. The sermon
2. The children's sermon
3. The announcements
4. The prayers

Your priorities might be different, but the old saying "there is only so much time" certainly comes into play when you prepare for Sunday morning. Remember that the more you speak freely from prepared material the better.

OUTSIDE THE WORSHIP SERVICE

As pastors we often speak outside the worship setting. You can use the Process Preaching System in the following areas of congregational life:

1. Lectures and Bible studies – Speaking freely comes easier when we lecture than when we preach. When preparing to lecture or lead a Bible study, most pastors write a manuscript or elaborate notes.

These presentations, however, are seldom rehearsed. Adding rehearsal to the preparation process would greatly enhance a lecture or Bible study. Since they are more informal, lectures and Bible studies don't require as much rehearsal as a sermon. Typically, good notes will enable us to speak freely after one or two run-throughs.

2. Reports – Pastors often give reports at congregational and council meetings when they need to inspire and direct the people. I always wrote out my annual report to the congregation and rehearsed it well. This is a key moment when people need to know you mean what you say.

If you have a difficult or controversial subject coming up at a council meeting, it helps to write out your thoughts on the subject. You may not have to speak at the meeting, but putting your thoughts into writing will prepare you for whatever comes your way. If you run through what you have written, you will be particularly prepared for your meeting.

3. Slide presentations – With the advent of computers, digital cameras, and projectors, slide presentations have regained popularity. When making a slide presentation you can use your slides as your notes. For example, if you show slides of a trip, each slide helps you remember a particular story. Running through your slides a few times will help you speak freely and greatly enhance your presentation.

Making a few notes before the run-through process will help you remember place names and other trip details. Remember to do your run-throughs within 24 hours of your presentation. Even with the powerful visual imagery of a slide presentation, you can forget important details if you have not reviewed them recently.

4. Power point presentations – Power point presentations have become very popular. In a power point presentation the slides once again become the manuscript. Be sure to avoid potential pitfalls such as the following.

a. Keep the slides as simple as possible. Don't fill them with rows of bullet points and lots of text. A power point presentation is first and foremost an oral presentation. The slides simply make what we say more effective.

b. Keep the number of slides modest. I have seen power point presentations with over a hundred text-rich slides. You will lose an audience in a hurry doing this. Keep in mind that your spoken words still do most of the work.

c. Slides with visual imagery rather than words work better for power point presentations. You can use photographs to good effect in these situations. For example, if you are making an appeal to the congregation to hire a youth director, you could show pictures of your congregation's youth. You can still talk about the reasons for having a youth director or the financial challenges of the project while you show photos of your youth in action. With image-rich slides you may wish to write more notes. This will help you remember what you planned to say about each slide.

d. Like all oral presentations, you run through your presentation at least three times in order to speak it freely. You can do your oral rehearsals in sections, going over each slide or group of slides three or four times. You can wait until the moment of delivery to put everything together.

OUTSIDE THE PARISH

Pastors are often asked to speak in different settings outside the parish. Here are some examples:

1. Nursing home and care center services – Preaching or giving devotions at a care center presents a good opportunity for speaking freely. The personal touch goes a long way in this setting. These services are a good place to hone your speaking freely skills.

2. Interviews – The personal interview has become a very important part of the call process in many churches. You can use the Process Preaching System to prepare for these interviews. Usually you can imagine the kinds of questions you will be asked. If you write answers to these questions and then run through your answers several times, you will be more fluent during your interview and less likely to say something you shouldn't.

3. You may want to speak freely in the following situations as well:

    a. Speaking to an issue at a convention or meeting.

    b. Doing devotionals at conference meetings, retreats, camps, or other events.

    c. Speaking on a panel presentation.

Often the writing that takes place for these non-sermon situations can be less formal or complete. Elaborate notes often suffice to guide you in your run-throughs. In the situations above, if you write out your material and also orally rehearse it, things will go well for you.

Chapter 11
Conclusion

Martin Luther writes to a discouraged young preacher: "If Peter and Paul were here, they would scold you because you wish right off to be as accomplished as they. Crawling is something, even if one is unable to walk. Do your best. If you can't preach an hour, then preach a half hour or a quarter of an hour. Do not try to imitate other people. Center on the shortest and simplest points, which are the very heart of the matter and leave the rest to God. Look solely to His honor and not to applause. Pray that God will give you a mouth and to your audience ears" (quoted in Meuser 58).

Preaching the Gospel presents a tremendous challenge. Few people in our culture prepare and deliver an original presentation every week. Teachers have lesson plans that can be used repeatedly. Newspaper columnists write new material weekly or even daily, but they do not deliver it before a live audience. Stand-up comedians move from place to place and do their routines over and over again. Late-show hosts do a monolog each night of the week, but they have 13 or 14 writers helping them. Candidates for political office have speechwriters, but they give the same or similar speech at each stop along the campaign trail.

Pastors have a very different situation. Each week we examine a text, select a theme, write an original sermon on the subject, and deliver it orally to our congregations. Meanwhile our listeners have high expectations for the Sunday morning sermon. They often critique our preaching. Parishioners in most Christian denominations continue to expect good preaching.

This makes for a challenging situation. Most pastors believe that preaching the Gospel stands at the center of our ministry. Men and women often go into the ministry in order to stand before a congregation of believers each week and challenge, enlighten, inform and inspire them with the Gospel. We consider it a tremendous challenge as well as a great joy and privilege to preach. Can preaching be that important to the Gospel of Jesus Christ? I believe that it can and that it is.

New Testament scholar Amos Wilder writes: "The rhetorical dimensions of the gospel were not just accidents or ornaments for making the message more pleasing or attractive. Rather, they were forms called forth by the nature of the Gospel itself. The coming of the Christian Gospel was in one aspect a renewal and liberation of language. It was a speech event, the occasion for a new utterance and new forms of utterance" (quoted in Long 29). Echoing this theme, Thomas Long writes: "Much of the Bible was in oral form before it was scripture. In other words, much of the Bible was preaching before it was scripture, and the biblical writings still show evidence of considerable attention to rhetorical dynamics and to what Robert Tannehil has called forceful and imaginative language"(28).

The idea that the Gospel event was a speech event and that much of the Bible appeared in oral form before it was written down helps us see why preaching remains central to the church. In the Gospel accounts, we read that Jesus "came preaching" (Mark 1:14) and that he sent his disciples out to preach (Mark 6:12). Ever since Jesus did that, Christians have taken seriously their responsibility to preach the good news of salvation and life.

Down through the ages, preaching has come in and out of favor in the life of Christian communities. It has, however, never been completely ignored or neglected. Martin Luther considered preaching to be at the heart of parish ministry. He devoted his life to promoting and improving preaching in the life of the Church. Luther's emphasis on preaching grew out of his conviction that God speaks through God's faithful servants. In a sermon on September 11, 1540 on John 4:9-10, Luther said: "Yes I hear the sermon: but who is speaking? The minister? No indeed! You do not hear the minister. True, the voice is his, but my God is speaking the Word which he preaches or speaks" (Plass 1125).

This idea that God speaks to us through others has remained a basic understanding of Christians in every age. In fact, it is an idea as alive today as it was in Luther's day. Henry Davis, a 20th – century preacher, expressed it well when he wrote: "If any human being is to hear God speaking, to him/her, he/she must hear through another human being, or many others, speaking the language of human beings, which is the only channel of communication open to us. This is just as true when one reads the Bible as when one hears the voice of a living person. Without these human words we could not have the word of God" (quoted in Aycok 190).

Both the Apostle Paul and Martin Luther spoke of preaching as foolishness. Luther considered preaching a very difficult task and often wished it to be less important. He did not appreciate the way people failed to listen to preaching or how they failed to respond to it by changing their lives. Nevertheless, he labored on in his preaching, believing it to be the chief way God chose to convey the Gospel. Like Luther, I believe that preaching should stand at the center of the work of every parish pastor.

The goal of this book has been helping pastors use their God-given natural speaking abilities to proclaim the good news of the Gospel with purpose and power. I believe that preaching and speaking freely in the extemporaneous mode is a very good way to do this.

Preaching freely is not just for the gifted few. Any pastor who wishes to preach freely *can do so*. No one is excluded from this powerful way of communicating. I have witnessed this fact over and over again in the classes I teach. I have seen pastors who never thought they could preach freely amaze themselves by doing it quite easily.

God has given those who preach an incredible responsibility and the gifts to go with it. May your particular gifts and abilities be used by God to preach the Gospel with ever-increasing purpose and power.

Works Cited

Aycok, Don, ed. *Preaching with Purpose and Power*. Macon: Mercer University, 1982.

Baddeley, Alan. *Human Memory – Theory and Practice*. Boston: Allyn and Bacon, 1998.

Bryant, Donald. *Fundamentals of Public Speaking*. New York: Appleton, 1960.

Davis, Ken. *Secrets of Dynamic Communication*. Grand Rapids: Zondervan, 1991.

Erdahl, Lowell. *Preaching For the People*. Nashville: Abingdon, 1976.

Fletcher, Leon. *How to Design and Deliver a Speech*. London: Chandler, 1973.

Gladwell, Malcolm. *The Tipping Point*. New York: Little, Brown, 2000.

Kling, Kevin. "The Rebirth of Kevin Kling." *Minneapolis Star Tribune* January 20, 2008: A1.

Koller, Charles. *How to Preach Without Notes*. Grand Rapids: Baker, 1997.

Litchfield, Hugh. *Visualizing the Sermon.* Sioux Falls: Hugh Litchfield, 1996.

Long, Thomas. *The Witness of Preaching.* Louisville: John Knox, 1989.

Meuser, Fred. *Luther the Preacher. Minneapolis*: Augsburg, 1983.

Plass, Ewald. *What Luther Says III.* St. Louis: Concordia, 1959.

Rogness, Michael. *Preaching to a TV Generation.* Lima: CSS, 1994.

Schacter, Daniel. *The Seven Sins of Memory.* Boston: Houghton Mifflin, 2001.